Even Tough Girls Wear Tutus

D0348834

—More Praise For *Even Tough Girls Wear Tutus*—

"Deborah's words cut to the raw and glistening bone of truth: that love is never lost if we have the courage, resilience and unremitting desire to seek it. Of all those whom Deborah comes to love, despite the circumstance of her prison birth, it is herself she finally loves last. And it is herself to whom she finally gives a spark of the unconditional love she has found for others. Here is the triumph, the testimonial to both bravery and vulnerability, rendered in words full with her fierce and indomitable spirit."

—Lorian Hemingway, author of *Walk on Water*

"This book defines what it is to be American, a woman caught in the whirlwinds of change, who finds the strength in herself to confront the challenges and overcome them. Wonderful."

—Jimmy Santiago Baca, (*A Place to Stand*; *A Glass of Water*; *The Importance of a Piece of Paper*, etc.) Pushcart Prize winner, American Book Award winner, the International Hispanic Heritage Award, The International Award

"Deborah Jiang Stein's *Even Tough Girls Wear Tutus* sings and soars, even as it knocks you out and takes your breath away. All you can do is sit back and watch the ride, like a scary movie where you know the bad guy is behind the door. Bravo."

—Martha Frankel, author of *Brazilian Sexy: Secrets to Living a Gorgeous and Confident Life; Hats & Glasses: A Memoir*

Deborah Jiang Stein has written the book she was born to write. *Even Tough Girls Wear Tutus* is an adrenaline charge of rebellion, forgiveness, and understanding that ultimately rejoices in the love a daughter has for every woman who has mothered her.

—Jessica Handler, author *Invisible Sisters: A Memoir*

"Deborah Jiang Stein's startling journey is impossible to forget. The ways this woman discovers herself, via the revelation of her birthmother in prison and her reconciliation with her adoptive mother, shows us how dramatically different worlds intersect, and why those intersections are so important to who we are. This is a powerful story."

—Piper Kerman, author of *Orange is the New Black*

"Deborah Jiang Stein's story is a tough and touching read. With unflinching honesty, she writes the progress of her life, navigating her way through the bewildering unknowns of adoption and being a multi-racial in a Jewish family. Deborah takes us on a harrowing ride through her never ending fight to learn who she truly is. This is strong stuff. But Deborah lays open her heart as she writes her story with candor and self-compassion."

— Sandra Benítez, American Book award winner; Orange Prize, nominee; LA Times First Fiction award winner; author of *Bitter Grounds*; *A Place Where the Sea Remembers*; *The Weight of All Things*; *Bag Lady*

"Deborah Jiang-Stein's life is a testament of the human spirit and redefines the courage and triumph possible within each of us. Her story is riveting as she takes the reader through the longing of the heart as well as into enormous depths of joy that will resonate for all."

—Sunny Schwartz, (*Dreams from the Monster Factory: A Tale of Prison, Redemption and One Woman's Fight to Restore Justice for All*, Scribner, 2009)

"Deborah Jiang Stein has an extraordinary story to tell, and she tells it compellingly. As the saying goes: The truest yang is the yang that is in the yin."

—Dr. Susan Schnur, Senior Editor, *Lilith* magazine

"Deborah Jiang Stein's return to the prison where she was born illustrates the potency of grappling with complicated beginnings. Her piercing honesty, intensity and humor are inspirational."

—Susan Livingston Smith, Program & Project Director, Evan B. Donaldson Adoption Institute

Even Tough Girls Wear Tutus

Inside the
World of a
Woman
Born in Prison

Deborah Jiang Stein

What Loss, Grief, and
Uncertainty Taught Me
About Joy

Cell7Media

Copyright © 2012 by Deborah Jiang Stein

The following material is constructed from what I, and
others with whom I've consulted, remember of the times
portrayed. The events described contain emotional truth,
the larger truth beyond the story, which is how memory
presented itself in my mind as I review the past.

No part of this publication may be reproduced, stored
or introduced into a retrieval system, or transmitted
in any form, or by any means (electronic, mechanical,
photocopying, recording, or otherwise), without the prior
written permission of both the copyright owner and the
publisher. We appreciate your support of the author's rights.

Cover and title concept by Betsy Gabler, Amita International.
Cover photo attributed to Anathea Utley, via Flickr.

Cell 7 Media, a division of Cell 7 Holdings LLC.
Cell7media@gmail.com

ISBN: 978-1-887345-50-7

For the 150,000 women in jails and prisons in the United States, and the 2.3 million children, most under age ten, with an incarcerated parent.

Acknowledgments

My thanks to:

My daughters who teach me about what matters in life.

All who believed in this story long before I started to write it. More editors than I can list dug their hands into this over a ten-year period.

Family and friends, too many to name without leaving someone out by mistake and then we'll all feel bad.

All who contributed finances, childcare, and peace of mind to my household during times when I stopped everything to write.

Early readers who believed in the book and in my potential from the very start.

Facebook and Twitter friends and followers for your love and support as you rooted for this book and my story, and for your encouragement of my on-going prison tours and the women inside.

Two women, without whom this book would not exist. For Mother, nothing but love and respect for such courage and stamina. For my mother in prison who handed me this story to write, I'm most often speechless with gratitude and admiration.

For more about Deborah Jiang Stein:

Facebook
facebook.com/deborah.jiang.stein

Twitter:
@deborahdash

The unPrison Project: Freedom on the Inside
A 501(c)3 nonprofit
theunprisonproject.org

Contents

Introduction

Some people end up in prison. My life begins inside a prison, a five-by-eight-foot room, my first home for a year. This book is a piece of my story, about the ravages caused by secrecy, shame, and stigma, and what happens when opposites tug inside. All which led me to a bigger truth— not everything in life can be reconciled.

Before I discovered this truth I had to learn how prison doesn't always mean behind bars, and locked up isn't just inside a jail cell. I needed to recognize where my own limitations imprisoned me, and how fear and uncertainty can often confine and immobilize a person.

Freedom came with finding courage, curiosity, and purpose in life, and doing good things for others. This freedom also showed me the deeper meaning of whimsy and sheer joy. Even in small things. Like a tutu.

The tutu appeared in my life when I first took dance lessons as a girl. It transformed over a span of years into more than the rustle of tulle and into a symbol of liberation, curiosity, and discovery. I first needed to accept and integrate the truth of what I learned in a letter one day when I was around twelve.

Chapter One

The Letter

Sweat glues my palm to the brass knob on my parents' bedroom door.

It's an off-limits, by-invitation-only room, sacred like a boudoir. We kids didn't dare go in on our own. Until today.

It's my first breaking and entering.

Mother grounded me for some violation I can't remember. She insisted Jonathan, my older brother, and I call her the formal Mother. We're both adopted. I wanted to call her Mama but couldn't let the softness out.

What else does a twelve-year-old girl do when she's grounded but sneak around the house?

I listen a second to make sure I'm alone, then grip and twist the knob. A ray of Seattle's noon sun slants through the glass of the patio door on the far side of the room. I'm glad for the door. Good thing my dad just fixed the sliding device. Short on patience, he wasn't much of a handyman. Things broke in his hands more than got repaired.

If they come in, I'll slip my slim five-foot frame out the sliding door and escape.

Check the dresser! For no reason other than I'm not supposed to pry into my parents' belongings, something drives me to do whatever I'm not supposed to do. I creep across the room, around my parents' footboard, and face my mother's dresser, tucked next to her nightstand where a bird book, two novels, and three volumes of poetry pile high against her alarm clock. Her quick-fire brain keeps her engaged in no less than three or four books at the same time, each one bookmarked midway.

Her snap-on earrings and a strand of pearls scatter on top of her dresser. If it weren't for her tray of Chanel bottles and her collection of perfume atomizers under my nose on the dresser top, I'd pinch my nostrils to block out the reek of my father's pipe tobacco in the room, an extension of his office at the university and his writing studio out back.

Pages of his manuscript, typed with scribbles of notes scattered in the margins, and a mechanical pencil on top, always cover his nightstand. He keeps the top of his chest of drawers bare except for a tray of pipe and cigar paraphernalia—always a Zippo lighter, pipe cleaners, a box of wooden matches, a pipe damper, and an Italian leather box, gold fleur de lis engraved on the outside. Inside, his Italian cufflinks crafted in gold, silver, and leather jumble together.

I slide my mother's top dresser drawer open.

"Shhhh," I whisper and grab Kittsy, our Siamese, to quiet the rattle of her purr. When I set her down she weaves in and out between my feet, her tail in a fast flicker around my ankles. The purr and her tail sweeping across my skin comfort me. She's the calm of my nighttime monster dreams when she nuzzles on my pillow, her belly curved around my head, her almond-shaped eyes more like mine than anyone in my family.

The scent of Mother's French soap collection wafts out of her drawer. She collects soap bar rounds the size of silver dollars wrapped in parchment paper to perfume her drawers filled with neat stacks of folded underwear and stockings bunched in a pile at the back.

I glance through the sliding glass door. Nobody in sight. Outside, my mother snips dead tulip heads and prunes in her rose bed. My father's secluded in his study out back, a room connected to our detached garage. He's always hunched over a manuscript about John Donne or Milton, deep in thought with long puffs on either a Cuban cigar or one of his pipes. Jonathan hot-dogs on his bike somewhere in the neighborhood with his friends. He's older by eighteen months and never in trouble. He leaves the back talk and smarty-pants to his little sister.

Nothing here. I nudge the top drawer closed to move on to the one below but a corner of white catches my eye. A crisp white piece of paper peeks out from under the pink drawer liner, plastic printed with miniature roses.

I peel up a corner of the liner.

I unveil a copy of a typed letter only a paragraph long, lodged under silky slips and parchment-wrapped bars of soaps, under softness and the scent of perfume, stashed like a rumpled stowaway in a first-class cabin.

Must be important if it's hidden. I already know I'm adopted so it can't be about that. Maybe it's about my race, or races. No one's explained to me why I'm brown in a white family, why my skin is caramel colored, often a sienna brown from the sun. Could this letter answer the mystery?

My neck throbs, boom daboom, my pulse in a loud pump of anticipation all the way into the muscles in my shoulders. High and tight as usual, my clenched shoulder blades draw my neck into a constant ache.

"Can you please alter Deborah's birth certificate," my mother asks in the letter to the family attorney, "from the Federal Women's Prison in Alderson, West Virginia, to Seattle? Nothing good will come from her knowing she lived in the prison before foster care, or that her birthmother was a heroin addict. After all, she was born in our hearts here in Seattle, and if she finds all this out she'll ask questions about the prison and her foster homes before we adopted her."

I read the letter over and over, these new truths imprinted into my memory.

My spine tightens as if someone just jammed a rod down it.

Impossible. Read it again. Everything blurs.

Foster care? I had no idea about anything before my adoption or even how old I was at the time or where I lived before then.

I step back a few paces and sink into the folded comforter at the end of my parents' bed.

Prison?

Born in prison? No one's born in a prison.

The worst word, the worst place, the worst of the worst: Prison.

I tuck the paper back under the liner and walk from the dresser into my parents' bathroom. I end up in front of the mirror over their sink, my body in overload. Time and space distort inside me. I don't know where I am. It's as if my feet lift from the earth, my body and brain separated by some wedge where I'm suspended in mid-air, disconnected from my house, from my neighborhood, from earth, from humanity.

It can't be true. How am I lovable if it is true? Who loves anyone from prison? If people find out my secret, then what?

My skin itches as if tiny ants crawl along the bones in my forearms and I scratch so hard, red streaks rise on my skin. I splash water onto my burning face but give up. None of it washes away what I know isn't there, but I think I'm coated with grime on my cheeks, hot to my hands. I can't stop splashing my face to get rid of the gritty scratch in my eyes and to rinse the sourness in my mouth.

Born in prison? Nobody's born in prison.

Then something sinks in. My "real" mother's an addict and criminal. My "real" home is a prison.

While I don't understand until decades later, the trauma of learning about my prison birth sent me into a deep dive, an emotional lockdown behind a wall which imprisoned me for almost twenty years. The letter forced me into an impossible choice between two mothers, two worlds far apart. One mother in prison, behind bars, a criminal, a drug addict, a woman who tugs at me, her face and voice, images and her sound buried deep in my subconscious. The other mother, the one I face every day, the one who keeps fresh bouquets of flowers on our teak credenza. I don't connect with this mother.

I'm not hers. Not theirs.

It's the first and last time I read the letter, and I've never seen it again. I don't need to, for every word is imprinted in my brain and it's given me all the proof I need. I'm not the daughter of the mother and father who toss Yiddish quips back and forth, the mother who spends her Saturday afternoons throwing clay with a pottery teacher, then comes home with darling miniature ceramics vases. The mother who writes poetry with a Mont Blanc fountain pen and uses the same to correct her students' papers, the mother who cans cherries and whips the best whipped cream ever. The mother who says, "I love you, Pet," so many times I want to smack her. The mother I remind more days than not, "You're not my mother anyway," as I push her away when she tries to hug me.

The mother who waits for me in my ballet training every Saturday.

Don't think about it. It's not true, none of it happened. Not even the letter.

Some things we need to unthink and erase, just to keep living. To even stay alive. But the secrets we bury stay with us forever, glued to our insides like sticky rice.

Everything moves in slow motion as if on a conveyer belt at dinner the night of the letter. The voices of my family sound faint, like an echo far away. I forget I've ever read the letter, forget everything in it. Gone. Zip. Out of my mind and never shows up until another flash in another month. Maybe not a month, maybe eight. I forget this too. It never stays in my brain or anywhere inside me long enough for me to grasp it, but something this big can't hide for long.

I convince myself, "If I don't think of it, then it's not

true. It never happened. I never read the letter. I wasn't born in prison."

But that doesn't mean it's not there. It seeps out of me like poison trapped in the pus of a balloon-sized blister.

My life-long battle begins when I force my brain to divorce from reality. It's the only way to metabolize what I've just learned. *I was born in prison.*

Chapter Two

Battle of the Tutu

At least three times a week throughout the entire year, my teacher sends me to the office. One day I pull the fire alarm, another day I hide above the false ceiling tiles and jump on top of my teacher. Bits of sheetrock rain down on her as I thump on her desk. Another day I sit on a boy's lap in the first row of class. A different day, I wave the blue-gold flame of my stolen Zippo lighter, my favorite score from my parents' bedroom, over crumpled wads of paper towels in the trashcan in the girls' bathroom and torch the toilet paper rolls. I pull the fire alarm. No false drill this time.

All the trouble I'm in makes me forget about the prison, forget the fact of my birthplace. It's gone. Inside, a river seethes, quiet and furious.

My gut's in a constant tangle and Mother drags me trip after trip to the doctor's office for my stomachaches.

"Nothing wrong," the doctor says on a visit.

It's one of the random days I remember I'm born in prison.

Nothing wrong? What about the big prison secret?

They're all crazy. Everything's wrong.

My mother doesn't miss a beat in her mission to groom me with refinement. Piano and French lessons, Hebrew in Sunday school, swim team workouts where I train in the butterfly and breast stroke, a two-week modeling class, and ballet on the weekend. Every Saturday afternoon from the time I'm in third grade my mother walks me down the street to the house at the dead end, where I spend an hour in the neighbor's basement at the ballet barre or sashaying across the oak floor in her homemade dance studio.

I love the freedom and silence of dance. The classical music, the meditation, and the athleticism ease a struggle I later learn relates to sensory integration issues often triggered in drug babies. The shiny varnished oak floor, the bright reflection of the sun on the mirrored walls, everything makes life better for the hour I'm cocooned in the studio filled with feet sweat and fluorescent lights. Most of all, I love my pink tutu and ballet slippers, love grinding the leather of my ballet shoes into the dusty box of resin.

Dance is my relief, an escape from the angst building in me about my feeling not normal.

But another battle begins. My demon taunts me: A girl born in prison doesn't twirl around in a tutu and pink tights and ballet shoes. This demon carries a fierce loyalty for my prison mom. The mom I need to find and follow.

I'm blessed with the exposure my parents give me. They take my brother and me to theater, ballet, modern dance, poetry readings, museums, and everything kooky and experimental in the arts. The magic of dance and mime touch my soul more than anything, then and now. I dream of theater and movement, mime and dance from the moment I sit in a darkened theater with my parents when I'm about eight and Marcel Marceau tiptoes on stage in his white ballet shoes and mimes inside an invisible box.

But I'm sure I don't belong in dance or theater. I'm a tomboy, and besides, the ballerinas on stage and in doll stores only have blonde hair. Not black wavy hair like mine, so thick it volumizes into troll doll hair when the humidity rises.

It's the 1960s, long before Alvin Ailey and Judith Jamison show the world ballet isn't just for white people.

How can I wear a tutu if my dance teacher—if anyone—ever finds out about my prison birthplace? I'm sure I'm the only one in the world ever born in prison, making me about as bad as a person can get. The more I keep my secret, the deeper I believe I am a bad girl, not good enough for anyone. I think being prison-born means I need to walk tough in the world.

A prison baby, especially a brown-skin one, doesn't wear a tutu. Definitely not a pink tutu. Tough girls don't wear tutus.

Chapter Three

Lucky

One summer when I'm around eight, before I find the letter, we drive across the country from Seattle to Lake Winnipesaukee, New Hampshire, to vacation with my aunts, uncles, and cousins on my father's side, his sisters and their families. My father grew up in Brockton, Massachusetts, and his two sisters remained on the East Coast, one in New Hampshire, the other in New York.

We spend a few weeks together, each family in our own modern log cabin, with a common clothesline, picnic table, and stone fire circle in a sandy patch in the middle of all our cabins. My two uncles, Peter and Marty, hold me in long bear hugs whenever I try to run past them on the way to the beach. Their knock-knock jokes, pranks, and bubbles of love bring me out of my shell. Silly is the farthest thing from my father the scholar, a professor of

John Donne and Milton, my father who flings a quick swing of his hand upside my head if something I do or say irritates him. Not always. Sometimes. He's unpredictable in his outbursts. But once is enough to live on edge and wonder: Will this call out his wrath?

I thrive around my uncles' playfulness, the same way I thrive with my mother's side of the family in Minneapolis. It's easier to let my guard down with both my extended families. They know exactly how to bring me out of my isolation, and it's simple: I just want to be hugged and to play, to be embraced as I am, not to perform or be proper, or reprimanded for my energetic and mischievous personality.

One afternoon, my cousin Dorrie races up to me in our cabin. She's like an older sister to me and born on the same day as my brother.

"You're lucky!" she says as she bursts through the cabin screen door, which slams behind her because she's run in so fast with her news.

"My mother told me you were chosen, said you're lucky because they had to take me just because I was born to them."

I stare at her and don't know what's lucky about me.

"You got picked," she says. "You're adopted." Then she adds, "Lucky."

This is the first time I've heard the word *adopted*. I don't have a clue what she's talking about or what this has to do with me. All I know is adoption means something about some kids have a first set of parents but I've never thought about why. No one has told me about my adoption so far and I've never put that together. Although I've already sensed something different about me, I don't know what and haven't figured it out. I can't understand why no one looks like me. I later find out I've lived in foster homes, all white, so I must've gotten used to people not looking like me.

I don't feel lucky. I feel sick in my stomach, tight inside like a rubber band ball the size of a bowling ball. Just then the screen door squeaks and slams again and my cousin Doug walks in with his wide smile. He always impersonates the *What? Me Worry?* character from *Mad* magazine and I usually giggle every time. But not this time. I stare off past him and walk outside into the sand towards the beach. Even then I find solace at a beach, anywhere near water.

I don't remember much after that. I never said anything to anyone. My usual lockdown took over, an instinct and habit from long before the shock of the letter. Any kind of trauma sent me into lockdown and I'd just move on. Only it's impossible to lock up just one experience. The fence I'd built around me now grew into a concrete wall with barbed wire at the top.

I waited until we were home from New Hampshire to pull out more details from my mother. Shortly after we return, I hunt down my mother out in the garden on a late Saturday afternoon. She's sleeveless and wrist deep in planting tulips, geraniums, and pansies, and yanking weeds, as usual for the weekend. The garden is the only "room" I like to share with my mother. I never let on how I admire her strength when she pounds stakes to prop up her plants or untangles a garden hose that whips around the yard as she sets a sprinkler near her shrubs.

"Am I adopted?" I ask my mother. A late afternoon mist moves in as the Seattle sun prepares to set.

I was never good at setting the stage or leading up to what I wanted to say, whereas my mother couched her speech with careful words so as not to hurt anyone's feelings. My bluntness frightens her.

"Yes. You're adopted." Her answer drops with a thump and sticks the way flour glues to wet glass. "And we love you." She digs lines of holes for tulip bulbs and doesn't stop to look at me.

That's it, all she says. Yes, you're adopted. I don't remember asking her any more questions or her saying any more. More lockdown. Inside I'm a swirl: Tell me everything! Who is she? My mother, my other mother, why didn't she want me? Where is she?

Silence waves in the air. I need her to say more but I don't know how to ask. I keep it all in. I hold my breath and gnaw the inside of my cheek, too afraid, too frozen inside to ask anything.

It's true. I have two mothers. Another mother somewhere else.

The final question pounds at my insides: Didn't she want me?

Most adopted kids wonder the same question. Kids simplify, and for adopted children, it goes like this, a belief in our rawest core: If our original parents want us, they keep us. If they don't want us, they give us away. This sat in me for decades until I could understand what happened had nothing to do with whether I was "good" or "bad." It took decades for me to unlearn my beliefs of "unwanted."

The deeper my mother digs in the dirt, the more hatred dredges up in me. Mother-blame sets in. I hate her for her brief answer, hate her for adopting me, and hate myself for being adopted. Nothing bothers me about the identity of my birth father. Not yet. So I don't need to push my father the way I do Mother. It's primal, the complex web and bond of a mother-daughter. All about my mother. It's as if a devil has taken my hand and dragged me to the teeter-totter, the devil a she-demon who weighs one side of the teeter-totter and won't let me down on the ground.

The unknowns scare me. Why didn't she keep me? Didn't she want me? If I love this mother, I think, aren't I betraying my first mother? But isn't she the one who didn't want me? I try not to think about this.

The more muddled I feel and the sadder I get about losing her, the more I hate and push away my mother.

"We love you," Mother adds, after she tells me I'm adopted. We're in the garden still.

Her solution to everything: "I love you, Pet."

I cringe every time she says those words, and with every hug I hate her more.

My first memory in my adoptive family is a recurring dream I had as a child.

It went like this: I'm looking down on myself right before sleep descends. Jonathan and I shared a bedroom as little kids, down the hall from our parents' room. The room is dark other than my nightlight by the roofless wooden dollhouse next to my bed. Just as my spirit is about to leave my soul and float around the world, I drift off, startled by a dream vision of five or so unrecognizable faces, women who surround me in a half-circle. We are in a room that's full of movement, a busier environment than the sedate atmosphere of my childhood home. In this mirage the onlookers' faces, sometimes visible and other times obscured behind vertical lines, peer down at me as I rest on my bed. Narrow wooden rods hide their bodies below the shoulder. I wake up soon after I fall asleep, the dream being so brief.

The same women stand around me every night. I'm not distressed but I feel crowded, my personal space invaded. I want to be alone. I wake up weepy in the middle of the night, not fearful about the dream but sad about its recurrence, the repetition of images I can't understand. I sniffle in the night so that no one will hear.

Jonathan, asleep in his bed on the other side of the room, has no idea what's going on. He's a hard sleeper and never hears me stir or cry in the night.

He's adopted at birth, almost two years older than I am and Caucasian. He didn't seem to suffer in the same ways I did and doesn't recall when he found out he was adopted. I didn't know he was adopted for most of my childhood. I never compared my appearance to Jonathan's other than I believed he was beautiful and I wasn't. I envied the ease with which he carried himself and his ability to mix in with the neighbor kids, his classmates—even my parents' friends.

Perfectly proportioned features and light olive skin gave him the look of the offspring of an Italian movie star, with all of the verbal and charismatic traits of a first-born. While my grades were sometimes higher than my brother's, Jonathan was an affable young man—the polar opposite of his moody, timid sister. I'm the one who stretched beyond the rules. If it was a rule, I'd hear it call out, "Break me."

Jonathan was a track star in school. He wore a confident attitude and fitted pants and t-shirts that showed off his muscles. We got along well but our musical tastes clashed. He played the Beach Boys and surfer music of the 1960s.

I cranked up Aretha, James Brown, The Temptations, Marvin Gaye, and Nina Simone.

My parents sent Jonathan in to comfort me whenever I was in the middle of a crying jag. He'd sit by my side, pat my back with his hand, and I'd calm down. As simple as that. The only thing I remember him saying is, "It's all right." Even though "it" wasn't all right, and I didn't know what "it" was, his tenderness helped—I knew he loved me.

The dream haunted me for years. I thought of it as my crib dream, the vertical line crib rods from my past. I couldn't shake the dream and even grew to expect it every night. After a while, the dream women at the edge of my bed stood like a wall between the world and me. They never left and I can't identify who they were. My brother and I moved upstairs into our converted attic bedrooms when I was about seven or so, and I never had the dream again.

After I unearthed the news about my prison roots, I wondered if my dream vision was from the Alderson prison with my birthmother and other inmates with the vertical lines iron window guards, not crib slats. Or was it a memory from one of my foster homes?

I have no idea if my mother heard me cry—from my bedwetting, even as a grade school girl, or from my angst about waking up in the morning with my thumb in my mouth when I wanted so badly to quit —but I knew she cared for me in the night. Many times after I woke up crying, I'd sit up, lean over the edge of my bed, grip my pillow so I wouldn't fall out, and feel around in the dark for a single graham cracker my mother would hide each night in one of the dollhouse rooms next to my bed. The tooth fairy also visited the same dollhouse rooms when I lost a tooth.

I knew my mother had slipped in after I'd fallen asleep to hide my cracker treat. When I discovered my treasure, I sat up in my bed and nibbled it, one hand under my chin to catch the crumbs. The crackers appeared night after night yet my mother and I never discussed this secret ritual. I locked my tenderness inside.

Memory can play tricks on us. Or do we trick our memory to serve a deeper purpose? Maybe I kept the dream alive so I could stay surrounded by the sensation of my prison mother.

The longer I kept my birthmother with me, the more I pushed away Mother, the one I need to love me and to love. The longer I kept myself outside my family, the more I stayed with the memory sensations of my first home in prison. I'd begun to glamorize my birthmother, romanticize our relationship, romanticize the prison, and whatever got her there.

I couldn't control any of it. The longing stayed with me, but I didn't know what I longed for.

Chapter Four

On the Edge

Spring leaps into the first day of summer, liberating me from sixth grade and still, no one's told me what race I am. But I can see I'm weird. Nobody I know is brown with white parents. It's before I found the letter and I already know I'm adopted but what else? Why am I brown? I need answers. I also crave adventure.

Away from the confines of my house and family, I'm emancipated and brave, not the timid, compliant, and sometimes mute little girl my family thinks I am.

One day I head to a neighbor's house across the street where they've just finished building a new ten-foot-high retaining wall. The wall hugs the back border between our house and the neighbor's yard. Mortar barely dry, it calls to me.

I tread across the dewy lawn and plant both feet firm on the concrete where the grass meets the top of the wall. The back of my heels hang into the grass.

Heights jumble my guts, but I'd do anything—even boost to the moon and back if I could—to soar on the hairline of fear and excitement. I leap. I fly. I drink in every blast of adrenaline as if my very life depends on it.

Inch forward, I tell myself. Then I lift a foot, ready to jut the toes of my red tennis shoes over the wall's edge. But my soles, still slick from the moist grass, slide, and the glide forward fires panic in me. My stomach pulls tighter.

My mother's words—you're one of us—words that boil my blood, suddenly disappear. It's magic. She's gone. My family's gone. My school and the kids and their ching-chong taunts as they pull their eyes at me, all gone. The world around me vaporizes and my head fills with the fervor of risk and fun: danger-fun. My whole universe right up to the edge of this second never existed. The rush of adrenaline drowns out everything else—my past, my pain, even the lock down. I'm at peace in the face of fear and excitement.

I slide up to my arches on the wall. Adrenaline rips through me and crackles my world open. I inhale the whole neighborhood—chlorine from my friend Wendy's pool next door; dog poop in someone's backyard; fumes from the Ferrari revving at the end of the block. It all mingles in my lungs and floods me as I teeter on top of the wall.

The crack of a baseball across the yard means Jonathan won't check on his little sister. No one notices me as I teeter on the wall. Exactly how I like it. I'm not here to impress anyone. I'd rather daredevil alone. Just the two of us together: danger and Deborah.

Petrified to even peek over the wall ledge, I pace back and forth on top across its six-foot width. Then I lean to gaze past the brink onto the hard-packed dirt below. The soles of my tennis shoes, now dry and squeaky, catch on the concrete. I stumble. Back away. My heart pumps and swells three sizes larger. Terror and excitement clash inside me.

Better sit. I plop on top of the wall and dangle my feet. I press my palms into the concrete nubs, bend at my waist to peer down, and dig my nail-bitten fingertips into the edge. There's not much to grip onto, so I push the heels of my shoes into a crevice in the wall to stabilize myself. Then I lean over further to gauge where the concrete meets earth.

Enough caution. Almost sick to my stomach, I pop up to my feet. I can hear my mother's voice: Be more careful, Dear.

Careful is not part of me unless I'm around my family, my teachers, or my mother—only then does caution seep into me like an oozy infection.

A few kids, mostly boys, have gathered below me. They dig in the dirt with sticks and fling pebbles against the wall. Behind them a swing-set sits empty. Lobed leaf ivy vines grip a fence. A songbird perches on top and flaps its wings in a dance to the da-da-da-dat da-da-da-dat jackhammer a few houses away. Another wall is under construction for me to jump from. Pretty soon a few boys from next door run over to join the kids at the bottom of the wall.

Enough caution. I squat down a bit as if to high dive off the end of a diving board. I swing my arms forward and fly, feet first. I whoop with glee and the kids below toss their heads back to look up. They all hoot and howl. One of the boys jumps up and down.

Do it again! I tell myself in the split second after I hit the dirt. I'm high from the flight and relieved to land, but hate how my feet have to ever touch the ground again.

Why can't I soar forever? Maybe I was born in the wrong body, meant to fly, not walk.

My courage balloons as the kids clap and cheer, egging me on.

"Anyone wanna try with me?" I ask my audience. No takers.

"You go again!" a boy shouts, and I race to the corner where the wall meets the house.

I march up the grassy slope. This time with no pause when I reach the top and without one look down, arms out in a perfect second position—a T—head high, in my longest stride, I step straight into space. Three quick steps of walking on air! Then, as it always has to end, I plummet down and land on my feet. Each succeeding jump grows duller, the only thrill left as I fly through the air, a flurry of snapdragons and purple and yellow pansies in the garden catch my eye. They beam their happy-smile faces at me. Beauty blurs with speed, but nothing equals the first thrill, alive on the edge.

I'll do anything to soar in the air and get this adrenaline rush. Something drives me to take risks, to jump from heights, from a tree, a wall, the small cliff down the street from our house, from on top of the swing-set in our backyard, a rooftop, the moon.

I need the high, the fire in me between fear and fun. It also helps calm the bounce in my brain.

It happens anywhere, but most often at school or at home. Ideas ripple behind my eyes as if a tsetse fly burrows there and infests my senses. Sometimes I can't connect thoughts in order. Then, it's free-for-all fun inside my head, but my wires spark wild and crossed. It can happen when people talk, when I write, or when I read. It can happen when I speak. My imagination chases a phrase somewhere and I might not come back in time to catch the next sentence. The flow, the meaning, sails away. Then I'm in sensory overload as sentences swim. My thinking turns into a cut-and-paste collage. Once I put the pieces together, I buzz in a hive of slow-motion static where I have to decode and unscramble key words, phrases, sentences. Everything combines to patch together the full meaning and find some sense. How can just twenty-six letters in the alphabet whirl up such pandemonium?

None of this is good with a scholar for a father who lectures us kids, not yet double-digit ages, in sentences a paragraph long and addresses us as if we're graduate students in his advanced seminar on Milton's *Paradise Lost*, the epic poem to which he devotes his entire career as a literary critic.

My teachers re-explain homework assignments until I understand. It just takes their patience and one extra try. Or two tries. Or five. I don't always let on when I need help. Sometimes I just pretend I understand.

Whenever a teacher stands next to my desk and drapes her arm across my back, I lean an inch closer to her side and breathe easier because my lungs fill with a puff of billowy clouds. My insides shift and the taut rubber band ball in me bounces out, at least for the moment.

If a teacher has her arm around me, for a change, I love it when she tells me what to do. I'm starved for physical affection since I won't let my mother get close to me. I want my teachers to take care of me and make a silent vow to them: I'll always do what you want and promise to follow rules. I'll be good as long as your arm comforts me. I long for an arm on my back like this forever.

Chapter Five

Go to Your Corner and Come Out Fighting

I grew up at my father's side for Friday night fights on television. I'd plop my sixty-pound skinny self in a chair next to my father, his six-foot-four frame sprawled on the couch. My mother hated the violence of boxing, and Jonathan preferred his model cars or the solitude in our bathroom where he'd set up his art studio to paint watercolors.

I looked forward to the fights, a time to sit with my father without having to talk. I loved the sound of boxers' feet smacking the canvas in their dance. The bell, the referee's modulated announcements, the yelling ringside crowd on television, the deep breathing, sweat raining down their faces, the Vaseline dabbed on open wounds between rounds, and the piercing pound of glove smacks. It all made me want to box, get in the ring and fight, burst out in an explosion.

After the ref's opening, "Now touch gloves, then go to your corners, and come out fighting," my father's running commentary on the rounds was the one time the boom in his voice didn't alarm me.

"Good right!" he'd shout, as if we sat ringside and the boxers could hear him.

"Keep 'em up!" he coached a weary boxer to raise his gloves and protect his face, then, "That's it! Wear him out. Just keep 'em up!"

My father boxed as an amateur when he was young, his lanky and lean less-than-two-hundred-pounds perfect for the sport. He believed in the balance of exercise to complement the hours he spent in mental discipline. He taught me what I now practice: that all work and no play or exercise and activity might make us dull.

My father and I shared another routine—jaunts to the Pike Place Market in downtown Seattle on the edge of Puget Sound to shop every Saturday morning for our fish and vegetables. We wandered the open market stands where fishermen peddled their fresh catches and farmers and their families sold crisp fresh vegetables, moist from the washing.

I rarely saw anyone who came close to features resembling mine, so I fit in at the market with the Asian and Mexican farm families who sold fruits and vegetables.

Each Saturday we drove past the homeless scattered across the grass in Market Park along the waterfront, men and women slouched from either hunger or alcohol. On one Saturday trek to the market, we passed a swarm of men in a food line. They waited in stiff procession in the damp Seattle chill.

"No matter what," my father told me, "for dignity, for the challenge of life, do the best at whatever you do."

This is one of the only conversations with my father I recall from my childhood. More like the only sentence. My lockdown so cemented in me at the time, I have few recollections of conversations with him, or with anyone else for that matter.

Even though I sometimes thought my father an intellectual snob and arrogant academic, I admired his humanity, his instinct to help those in need. Both my parents lived in a strong Judaic tradition of helping others from the Talmud: "It is not your job to finish the task, nor are you free to avoid it all together."

I have a vague memory of my mother volunteering to tutor reading with inner-city school kids. I can't recall specifics, but I remember my parents and their friends in day-to-day dialogue about the 1960s civil rights movement, and I only know they favored whatever group felt oppressed, and condemned the privileged, whoever dominated. It took me a while to put together how my adoption might fit into their liberal leanings. When the thought first struck me, I don't know if I accused them to their faces or just kept it inside: I was sure they'd adopted me as a social statement, a souvenir of their liberal principles.

The street corner preachers near the market fed my early fascination with spirituality and ways of worship, although we weren't a worship-filled family. I grew up with a broad religious exposure. My mother more than my father was an observant Jew. She sent my brother and me to Sunday school, she lit Sabbath candles, we said grace every night in Hebrew, and attended synagogue only on the Jewish high holidays. I grew to understand Judaism more as a culture than a religion.

One Saturday when I'm in middle school, after the market with my father, I charge down our driveway to climb into my secluded galaxy of boards, my tree house I've built from scrap wood in our garage. It's nothing but a platform of plywood and two makeshift windows with a wide plank for a door.

I listen a few minutes to the wind speak through the fir treetops, then peek out onto the quiet and steamy street below. It's another day of drizzle. Suddenly I remember Persephone, my puppet from my third grade school play, and the flour-water paste and glue our class stirred up to make our puppets. We were living in Rome, Italy, for one of my father's sabbatical years. Before the school year started in Rome, my brother and I spent a summer at camp in Devon, in southwest England while my parents travelled separately, my father lecturing in Poland and my mother off to sightsee in Edinburgh. I kept at my pranks and mischief even in another continent. In Devon I bought a miniature pocket knife which I still have in my trinket display to this day, along with the scar from a slash across the meaty side of my right hand when I sliced myself in some knife trick I can't remember.

In Rome, my teacher assigned a Greek goddess to each student and we conducted a play with our puppets. Looking back, it's funny how my childhood puppet was the mythological Persephone, goddess of Hades, when the underworld sat right around the corner from me, when my mission in life would be to raise hell.

Flour and water, paste and glue. I scramble down my ladder and charge home to grab a bag of flour, then lug it up to my tree house.

Just as I hit my platform, a sports car rounds the curve at the edge of our neighborhood. When the driver steers toward the street below my tree house, I rip open one corner of the flour bag.

Why pour?

The sports car speeds through the drizzle on the wet street below and just when its headlights reach underneath my tree house, I fling the whole bag of flour out my window.

Victory! Fluffy white powder breaks loose from the bag and sails like an unformed high-speed cloud. The rest of the bag explodes on the hood of the car. Poof! All over the windshield.

Perfect science learned from my puppet. Windshield wipers make paste with a wet windshield and a one-pound bag of flour.

No time to celebrate. The driver slams on his brakes and pulls over to the shoulder. As fast as I can scramble, I make it down my tree house steps and dart home across our lawn. I sneak upstairs to my bedroom just in time to overhear a pound at the front door.

My mother's with my brother at a swim meet. Dad answers the door.

"One of your kids poured flour on my Ferrari," the neighbor's voice booms downstairs.

"Deborah! Downstairs! Now!" my father shouts.

He starts in with, "Why did you . . . ?" but before he finishes his sentence I blurt, "Haven't been in my tree house all day." I spin around and march back upstairs, no footsteps behind me.

The neighbor storms out. No proof. I'm an uncon-victed

flour bag thrower, the bad girl I believe I was born to be. Now I just have to live up to it.

The whole affair feeds my taste for thrill and adventure. The scheming, the big flour toss out of my tree house, the giant poof of flour into paste, the chase, and then the final con in the face of both my father and our neighbor. All a hint into a craft I'd perfect later on—the art of defiance, the excitement of living on the edge. Far from my mother's "don't stir things up" way of life. She hated any kind of discord. Even though she had a fierce will, like many of the women of her generation, she restrained her voice. Her mother, my grandmother, had emigrated from the Poland/Lithuania region after World War II and like other first-generation Americans, my mother strived to blend in, not to stand out. Her motto in life: Be nice.

My motto: Defy and stir things up.

Chapter Six

The Duets

Even though Mother kept her day-to-day life within the rules, what a pioneer she was to adopt me, a multiracial girl, in a time when our country was still segregated. I wish I could ask her about this but I can only speculate. What I know for sure is she wanted a daughter at all costs, even the one who rejected her year after year.

My mother's high energy kept her in constant motion. I'd walk in the door after school and there she was, scurrying around. She'd move a vase of flowers in the living room from one end of the credenza to the other, then dart over to the other side of the room and re-stack a pile of books on the coffee table. Half the time I never knew why she scooted from room to room. Active, intense, and intent on getting things done, she was only still when she read, often every night after dinner. My mother couldn't get enough learning, with her insatiable curiosity to explore books, museums, and music. She yearned to get her Masters and as I got older, on several occasions she shared her disappointment about how she never finished her thesis on James Joyce's Ulysses. "Maybe I'll go back some day," she'd say.

Most days when I came home from school, Mother paused from organizing the kitchen countertop and as soon as she saw me she'd pop two slices of white bread into our stainless-steel toaster. She'd pull out a jar of her homemade raspberry jam from the refrigerator while we waited for the bread to turn dark brown, the way I liked it. My brother and I picked raspberries from the patch behind our house. Jonathan ate his raspberries as he plucked them off the bush, while I tried to collect as many as I could in my pail. I loved to wear the berries like crowns on my fingers. Sometimes we ate them fresh with cream. Mother boiled what was left for jam.

We sat on kitchen stools with our toast, silent together, and munched on our late-afternoon snack. Our crunches synchronized in a kind of music but as soon as I relaxed a little with our closeness, something took over, like a thorny fist in my gut. I'd walk away, off to the solitude of my room and leave her to sit alone, a piece of my half-eaten toast and a dollop of my favorite raspberry jam on my plate.

Guilt took over and deep down I felt compassion for her but I couldn't help myself. The jam knife clunked into the sink and our ceramic toast plates clinked as my mother stacked them into the dishwasher. I felt even guiltier with the sounds of her cleaning up.

My mother was always proper. Just under five feet and petite but sturdy, she sat with her hands on her lap, ankles crossed, her brown eyes alert and eager with curiosity behind her glasses. She was soft-spoken with the sharpest wit I've ever known. We shared an in-the-moment intensity but not much else. She always looked complete, a well-wrapped, petite yet sturdy package. Although she claimed she was five feet tall, I found out later that was a stretch when I grew past the five-foot mark.

My mother wore the pain I caused on her soft round face, but her mouth curved into a slight smile most of the time. She told me to try and look interested or happy— even if I wasn't. Fat chance.

She made sure she put herself together well with

clip-on earrings and her soft brown hair pulled back. She dressed in Italian wool tailored suits that accentuated her slim waistline, with a silk scarf draped around her neck to highlight her light olive skin. Her elegance and reserved demeanor embarrassed me. I wanted a more stylish mother, a 1960s mod woman. Even though I yearned for a mother who looked more like me, since I couldn't have that, I wanted one who looked more like other mothers in the neighborhood—tall, blonde, and hip like Peggy Lipton in the Mod Squad.

She just wouldn't stop, no matter how much I pushed her away. My mother took a class in "new math" to help me with my homework when I reached the age with more advanced math in elementary school. I excelled in math and spelling as much as I tried not to. Once in a while at dinner my parents quizzed us on what we were learning in school. My brother strived to be the winner in everything, but he wasn't the best speller, and I blurted out the correct answer as fast as I could just to better him. Most often, though, something pushed me to want to fail. My parents reminded me I was intelligent and above average, yet I hated their approval . . . and sometimes secretly wanted it.

Music stirred some magic inside me, loosened the rubber band ball in my gut. I'd taken lessons since I was six or seven. Sometimes my mother called me over to her stool at the piano. This started a few years after I'd read the letter. She'd open her music book to my favorite duet, Beethoven's Moonlight Sonata, with its mysterious and haunting melody.

We'd play together without speaking, and if my fingers got ahead of hers, she'd stop, release the metronome so I could better keep tempo, then we'd begin again.

I forced myself to focus on the music because if I didn't, I'd lose my place and wander off, hypnotized by the metronome's click click click click. The pressure of my father behind us across the room, where he scribbled on a manuscript or read a book, didn't help my concentration either.

I loved this piano ritual with my mother, and I loved her in those moments, loved sitting at her side, her skillful fingers on the keys, her sophisticated perfume wafting around me.

But after one or two pieces, I'd had enough. Enough tenderness with her. I could only take it in small doses. A person needs to open the door for any love to seep in.

She wanted to play a second, even third tune, but I couldn't go on, couldn't stand the collision in my gut.

I put words in my head to name the tangle inside about our piano duets. This is not what a girl born in prison does.

I could never shake the pictures in my head, the flashes of images in my imagination about women in denim or khaki, behind bars, images induced by television of inmates surrounded by stern-faced prison guards with a hollow echo of steel doors slamming in the background. Images induced by television, cartoons, magazines, and newspapers.

A girl born in prison does not play Bach or Beethoven duets with her mother. In the middle of a duet with my mother, I'd slide my chair back and take off to my room. Solitude, always my redeemer. It's easier to ignore the world and everything wrong with it when you build a wall of isolation. The down side: it's harder for what's right and good to get inside.

Chapter Seven

From the Back of the Bus

The summer before I enter sixth grade we move to Bellevue, Seattle's latest upscale suburb, into our second house, a contemporary rambler with a fire-engine-red door. It is just months before I find the letter.

On the bus ride home from my first day of sixth grade, I sit in the back, the first one to board, and take the coveted center seat in the last row bench. The mid-afternoon sun beats down on the seat, golden rays warming the back of my legs. I settle in and one by one the other kids file into the seats in front of me all the way down to the last seat behind the driver. Someone's leftover open banana in a lunch bag fills the air and its fruity scent distracts me from the noisy chatter. Relieved no one sits by me, I stare out the window, glad the first day of school has ended. Meeting new people is hard for me. I'm not quick to make new friends, always sure I look odd and might get teased about my brown skin and racially ambiguous features, different from my classmates and other kids in the neighborhood.

My bus stop's one of the first. I peer down the long bus aisle and through the driver's window, our row of mailboxes ahead over the horizon, at the top of our lane a block away. Just when the bus rattles to slow down for my stop, my gut tightens. I hadn't had the foresight to plan ahead and sit close to the door for a quick exit.

Now I have to walk down the long aisle past the rows of kids, all their eyes on me.

I stand. The bare skin on the back of my thighs sticks to the rough plastic. A quick flip of my hand behind me flings my skirt down. My mother had insisted I change out of my jeans into a skirt for the first day of school.

I brace myself, fingers wrapped on the steel bars above the seat backs to my side, then grip the back of every other seat—left, right, left, right—down the aisle to steady myself from the bounce of the bus and from my panic. All eyes turn up to me.

The only time I love attention is when mischief calls my name, and then every bit of attention sends a thrill through me. Otherwise I hate when anyone looks at me.

I bite the inside of my cheek to gather strength.

What was I thinking? They're looking at me!

Nothing else to do. Keep walking.

Halfway down the aisle I hear a girl's voice behind me.

"Nigger," she whispers in a tone soft enough so the driver won't hear but loud enough to reach my ears. My stomach clenches even more and the thought flashes through me: I don't even know what I am and you're calling me that?

I never cry in public, but I want to collapse and bawl, run and hide. To be gone forever. I instead pull my back straight and as tall as my four-foot ten-year-old frame can stretch, bite harder into the inside of my cheek, and hold my breath. Bite, hold breath, freeze. I'll spend twenty-some years in this lockdown position.

Drop your hands, I tell myself. I need to keep the brown on my arms and hands away from everyone. Just as the bus rattles to its stop, a second girl's whisper behind me breaks the silence. "Yeah."

I know it's coming this time, bite deeper into my cheek to prepare.

"Nigger," she says.

Spin around, smack those girls, knock out their every tooth, smash their pointy noses.

But I never turn, never say anything other than inside my head. I hate myself, hate that my parents are white, hate that I'm not, and hate not knowing my race or what I come from. I detest myself. I'm a mishmash like no one else.

By the time the hydraulic door gasps, my rage and pain have hardened into a deeper lockdown. I run downhill on our quarter-mile lane, past the other houses, past the field of tall dry grasses, and home to the bottom of the lane.

I barge into the house a sweaty mess, my cotton skirt stuck to my thighs, my t-shirt glued to my back, and an ache buried deep in my heart. My mother bustles in the kitchen, wiping the countertops over and over, probably to collect crumbs and spills from her elaborate gourmet preparations.

The lavender of Earl Grey lingers in the air, and classical music turned low on her radio feeds something ill at ease inside me but I don't know what yet. I don't yet know I'm feeling myself in a forced servitude inside a world of arts and civility, tea and classical music, hours on hours of traipsing around the Seattle Art Museum, when my instinct wants to run wild and play and prank. Prancy by nature. At the same time I find peace in art and music. Our family ritual of tea at night is way too civil. I can't find the right track to follow for how to live, how to act.

I stumble into the kitchen, still out of breath from my dash home. Sponge in hand, my mother turns to me for a moment, smiles and says, "How was your first day, Honey?"

I'm too frozen for any words to leak out, shredded inside. But can't she tell?

I sit down on the fireplace hearth and press my fingertips into the cool stone of our slate hearth edge to keep me from smashing her with my fist. Mother sets down her sponge and buries her hands in the side pockets of her apron.

"How'd it go, Dear?"

I force my eyes to meet hers, choke back tears, and in an almost-whisper say, "Kids called me nigger on the bus."

I can't break down before my mother reaches out first. I yearn for her arms around me so I can fall apart against her chest. I wish I could melt into her. Into someone. Anyone. But I can't. Don't know how.

Her jaw muscles clench and release, as if I'm forcing her to talk about my race again. Forcing her to give me some facts about where I came from. All I want is a hug. Also, all I want is to shove her into the wall.

Before she can finish, "But you're just one of us, Dear, and we love you," I race down the hall to my room, slam the door behind me, and fall face first into my pillow and scream into it. Anything to get the venom out of my gut before I explode.

I rip into my cotton pillowcase with my teeth and bite the cloth so hard my gums hurt. By the time I'm done, my pillowcase is a shredded pile of strips.

I think I recall my mother coming after me into my room, but I was inconsolable. I gave up on the idea of ever having a mother. I was on my own.

She's one of them, I thought. White, and she won't understand. That day creates a wedge between us, which will take over a decade to dissipate.

Chapter Eight

BFD

My escapades in school escalate into fire starting shortly after I find the letter. One night after dinner while I'm helping clear the table, my mother takes my wrist and leads me down the hall towards Jonathan's room.

"I have something of yours to show you," she says.

Now what?

Jonathan's room is its usual clutter, a chaotic jumble of plastic model car parts, scissors, scraps of wax paper, glue toothpicks, decals. A clip-on desk lamp flexes low for his close-up detailed work. The opposite of my desk, which is covered with sheets of paper, pencils, and an assortment of my father's paper cigar rings. He peels them off for a special present before he lights up.

Mother unlocks a cedar trunk full of table linens and mothballs tucked way in the back of Jonathan's closet.

Her voice muffles behind the clothes: "I have something to show you."

Why's something for me in Jonathan's closet?

She pulls out a four-inch wool toy dog—coarse beige and pink yarn winds around wire. I stare into the toy dog's button eyes. What's this?

"Here." My mother holds out the toy. Her clenched jaw muscles pulse in and out.

"This is yours," she says. "Your birthmother made this. She sent it with you to your first foster home, and it stayed with you after that."

I wrap my fingers around the yarn toy. I'm touching what her fingers touched.

I want to feel the pulse of my birth mother through the yarn. The tiny button eyes stare back at me. She'd wrapped pink thread into a knot to make ears. Cut a sliver of pink felt and sewed it on for a tongue.

"Sent it from where?" I say to my mother's back. She's turned to look out the window. She lets out a deep breath. "It went with you from foster care and ended up here, with us."

It's the one and only time my mother ever mentions my

foster care. She doesn't know I've read about it in the letter.

"Where did my mother send it from?"

She whips around to face me and says, "I am your mother." Not in anger, but sadness, and it veils her eyes.

"I am your mother," she repeats, her voice soft and unsteady this time.

"I mean my birthmother, sent it from where?" I fight back tears. I can't tell her I know about the prison. Just can't. I need her to say it, to tell me I was born in prison, and the toy comes from there.

"Your birthmother loved you so much that she gave you up," my mother says, as if answering a different question.

I press the wool into my cheek, the coarse yarn against my skin, and want it to melt into me. Then I catch my breath for a moment at the thought of losing my other mother. I'm frozen, until the taste of blood inside my bottom lip snaps me out of it. I've clamped my teeth to hold myself back.

"Gave me up . . . why?"

Silence stirs the room, after which my mother replies with her standard answer. "We love you like you're ours."

"Gave me up . . . from where?" I insist. "Where is she now?"

Silence divides us.

"We'll love you forever, Deborah," my mother says again, but by then I've spun out of the room with the yarn toy. I lean on the wall down the hall from Jonathan's room and cup the yarn over my nose to inhale its softness, to pull in the wool scent beyond the cedar chest aroma.

Take me back, I think, and ache inside. Inhale again. I want to inhale my birthmother's scent. Nothing. I try again. Nothing.

I miss her, but don't know whom I'm missing. I want her in my memory.

As I bury one of my fingertips into a thin spot that bares twisted metal wire under the pink and beige yarn, my mother plucks the toy dog out of my hands.

"I'll take that now," she says and before I know it, my yarn toy is out of my hands. As she heads back into Jonathan's room, I march after her.

"That's mine," I cry out. "Can't I have my toy?"

Faster than I can grab it, my mother flips up the trunk lid to toss it back inside its coffin of mothballs and table linens, and locks the trunk. "This will stay here until you're older. I just wanted you to see it," she says as her hands flutter around in the clothes hanging in the closet.

"In case it helps," she adds.

Helps what? There's so much unspoken between us that I don't know what needs help. She'd attempted another "in case it helps" earlier that year and offered to buy me a horse. What was she thinking? It wasn't like I had horse posters plastered all over my room. I'd never mentioned horses. My friend Wendy, from our old neighborhood, rode horses so maybe my mother had some idea that horses make girls happy.

"That's mine!" I yell. "I don't care anyway," I say and try to sound cavalier. My toes grip the inside of my socks. I take a step closer. She leans back and remains silent as we stand face to face. "I don't care about you, Mother. Or anyone else."

I pause and take a deep breath to prepare for what I'm about to say out loud for the first time. "You're not my mother anyway."

My mother's soft brown eyes hold back tears as I push my face an inch closer to hers and turn my next words into three separate sentences.

I. Hate. You.

I storm away, leaving her alone. I feel guilty turning my back on her and hate her more, both at the same time. Rage and guilt replace my confusion, feelings only mischief make better.

One night at my parents' monthly cocktail party, I rummage through the mound of coats and purses piled high on their bed. I go into thief mode as soon as guests arrive.

I swipe a handful of quarters, a pocket comb, and a ballpoint pen. I can't help how I steal. The secrecy —and, even more, the fact I never get caught—incite me. The tug of guilt after gnaws at my insides but it's not enough to stop me.

The day after I swipe the Zippo, I discover what really thrills me more than what my mother says. "They're famous, you know," she likes to remind me about my father and his friends. Maybe what I steal belongs to Elizabeth Bishop or Robert Penn Warren, Gwendolyn Brooks, Robert Lowell, or John Berryman— all guests in our home at one time or another, the 1960s literati and heavy hitters, but I couldn't care less. The way my father explodes now, with smacks upside my head, who cares about his "famous" and his friends?

His temper often flares, more out of impatience with me.

One day my father's in the living room, settled in his chair, scribbling on pages of a manuscript. "Fuck you," I whisper when I pass by him on my way to the bathroom down the hall.

Mother overhears and scolds me. "Show respect!"

My father's size twelve Italian leather shoes clomp after me as I fly down the hall. He misses me with the chair he heaves at my head. It lands on the wood arm of our couch—the couch now in my brother's house, the dent still there. Other times he swings or swats me on the side of my face.

Not every day, not every week, I don't think, I don't remember, but once is all it takes for a smack from a six-foot-four man for me to learn to keep my fuck you inside my head.

I still flinch sometimes if I sense a swift arm movement near me.

I'm the only one in the family who riles my father like this and the only one in the family excited to watch boxing matches on television with him, which is the only time I'm not afraid of his giant paws. It used to be called discipline. Today it's unacceptable.

Some months after I've read the letter, at the start of seventh grade, I slurp down my usual half grapefruit for breakfast. I'm in my pajamas instead of all dressed in my usual cords and sweatshirt. A Seattle drizzle spatters the kitchen window.

On my dash back to my bedroom after breakfast, I grab my raincoat from the front door closet. I yank an oversized sweatshirt from under my mattress. I'd tucked it under there after an older eighth grade boy gave it to me for his "let's go steady" gift instead of a friendship ring. Nine-inch white-stenciled letters, BFD—"Big Fucking Deal"—stretch across the sweatshirt's maroon front.

There's no way Mother would ever allow me to wear any sweatshirt to school. Just the opposite, she grooms me like I'm an upper crusty debutante, even though we live on my father's slim English professor salary.

My buttoned raincoat hides the smuggled sweatshirt and I make it out of the house, onto the bus, and straight into my class. I'm the first to arrive and dart to the front sideline of the room. I lean against the teacher's shoulder-high open supply cabinet against the wall where she keeps blank paper, boxes of unsharpened pencils, and blue test notebooks.

The multi-colored map of the world tacked above the cabinet behind me boosts my courage with its pictures like the photos of our National Geographic at home. I belong in the map and the magazines with photographs of people from tropical countries and other continents more than in my white family. The map at school gives me a place where I can imagine myself, even though I can't say in what country or with what race I might belong, whether with Thai children with my same wide smile and lips or dark-complexion boys from Samoa whose skin color resembles mine. My nose is like those of people from the Philippines. Babies wrapped on their mothers' backs in China wear my eyebrows. I see my own feet in the photos of South American girls, their bare feet brown like mine. Sometimes I even recognize my skin tone in the pictures of light-skinned Africans.

My parents can't, or won't, discuss our racial differences, so how can I ever bring up my birth in prison?

Not until the 1970s did more than a thousand white families include adopted children of color. My pioneering parents had stretched out of the margins to adopt me. But whenever I ask my mother about my caramel-colored skin and button nose, about the hint of almond shape to my eyes, all different from my family, she just says, "I love you, Pet," her solution to everything, always. Then, as if it's punctuation, she adds, "You're just one of us, Dear."

I'm too scared to say a word, to tell her I don't feel part of anything.

In truth, there was no love big enough to cover the stigma and shame I felt about my prison roots. No love could repair the trauma I'd already lived by the time my parents adopted me, and traumas which followed, including: molestation by a few boys in the neighborhood, my father's rage attacks, and my emotional lockdown to get through it all.

I see myself everywhere in those magazines and the school and it helps settle the crazy inside me.

The bell rings. All thirty of my classmates file in and fill their desks. My heart pounds behind the BFD, and my teacher glares at me for a long second before she leans the small of her back against the front of her oak desk cluttered with stacks of our homework, then presses her palms flat on the wooden edges.

Here goes. I uncross my arms, chest open to flash my sweatshirt to class.

The noisy chatter snaps to a stop as if our school chorus conductor just hit a down stroke. A few kids giggle and some dive their faces toward their desks and pretend to write.

Now what? My timid self slips away.

"Deborah! Go to the office!" my teacher snaps.

We lock eyes. An adrenaline rush kicks in my gut.

"Go to the office? For what? I'm just standing here," I say.

I shrug my shoulders and lift my forearms waist-level, palms faced upward to the ceiling, fingers spread apart.

Now I'm in control. A sea of eyes shine on me, and we all wait for what's next.

Whose move is it now? Better do something.

I tug at the bottom of my sweatshirt, the creases stretch out, and with a flick of my fingertips, I brush off each of the three letters. I pretend to sweep away lint, then trace each letter with my fingertip.

My teacher pulls me by my wrist down the hall into the school office. I'm in for it, really in for it now.

"It just means Bellingham Fire Department," I say to the principal. "You know, Bellingham."

It's a town north of Seattle.

Adrenaline pumps more fear, more power, more risk into my heart, but I can't stop.

"Not big fucking deal," I add. "Not what everyone thinks, not that."

Jumping beans somersault inside my stomach. I'm scared but don't dare show I'm afraid.

The fun's over when the principal calls my mother to pick me up.

"What's the matter with you?" the principal asks while we wait. "You have a good home, two parents, what's the problem?"

Guilt sets in. He's right, I have all this.

I want to shout at him, Don't fuck with me, but can't. Those jumping beans now pole vault around inside.

Back home, I'm in my room. Grounded. Again. BFD.

More and more I fall into a well all by myself, a world with my own rules, a world where I'm convinced no one loves me, no matter how much and how often I hear it. Just because people tell us something doesn't mean we believe it.

I stash the pocket flashlight I've lifted out of someone's purse side pocket under my pillow. I've needed this to read. Up until now, when my parents think I'm asleep, I'd sit on a pillow under my bedroom window with the shade cracked, lean against my wall, and prop my Puffin Book of Poetry on my knees to read under a clear sky and bright moon. The Seattle night clouds limit my midnight reading, but with my new flashlight I can read in the comfort of my bed, buried under the covers.

The first time my mother catches me rather than scold me she asks, "Do you have a favorite?" She takes the book and reads from The Cow, the page where I've folded the corner.

"The cow mainly moos as she chooses to moo/and she chooses to moo as she chooses." She reads the whole poem, only four stanzas, two lines each, twice. Then I ask her to read it again, over and over several times the way I do under my covers.

"Keep the flashlight, Pet," she says as she tucks me in. She doesn't know I stole it. My stomach's in a knot from guilt. Even my constant nail-biting didn't help, a habit I carried long past high school.

On our annual Passover visit to my mother's family in Minneapolis, I can't help myself. I steal one shiny silver coin from my grandmother's silver dollar collection. No one gets me to giggle like my uncles with their Donald Duck impersonations. Even though I'm used to my father's more formal Deborah, I don't even mind that they call me their Little Debbie.

In seventh grade, I meet an older boy behind the gym after school. He hands me two crystal meth tablets. His eyes widen as I throw my head back, open my mouth, and swallow.

Within an hour I'm a 500-volt bulb, my every cell alive and at peace for the first time. I at last feel at home in my brown don't-know-what-race-I-am skin, my adopted-in-a-Jewish-family skin, my prison-born skin. I can't stand myself and hate everyone, beyond the usual teen angst. This rage and hate drive me to plot murder. Just in passing, but I give it more than a thought.

One afternoon in school, I draw a sketch with an older boy to scheme my parents' murder. I plan to snake a hose from the furnace into their bedroom and gas them in the night. But if I killed them, where will I live?

Selfishness, not compassion, stop me, with a fear I'd go back into foster care. I'm not conscious of my few years there, although somehow I imagine it's a stigma. Whether I heard this from other kids or saw it on television, I don't know. Even today, for most people, foster care brings up images of neglect and unwanted kids.

Mother and Dad, who never know about the plot, decide I need help. Just me. Not as a family, which we need.

I'm mute with the psychiatrists and psychologists because I'm convinced my parents have it wrong. They need help. I'd learned early on to go mute if I didn't like what I heard. Silence, my only power then, the only thing I could control: whether I speak or not. More often, I don't speak. Not one word. It takes me years to figure out how to use my voice, to speak up with my opinions and ideas, and open my emotions to others.

Better to take years to know the value and power of words and language and silence at the right time, than to spend a lifetime with no voice.

Chapter Nine

On the Fast Track

The country's in a civil right upheaval and I'm waging my own revolution at home. One day my mother and I argue. Again. It's daily. I don't remember about what. I'm in my senior year of high school in one of Seattle's all-girls Episcopalian prep schools. It's either this, which my parents sent me to in ninth grade, or reform school.

We wear uniforms, stand up when the teachers enter the classroom, and dine in a formal white tablecloth dining room. My graduating class consists of twenty girls. Other than I stand out in my all-white class, there's no way to get lost in the school crowd and hide the mischief.

Every molecule in me is packed with mad. I face my mother in the hall outside my bedroom. Her back is against the wall. We're now the same height, only I'm stronger. Against her just-under five feet, I'm lean and muscular, more athletic than her soft petite frame. A few summers before, I trained and raced on a swim team. My best stroke, butterfly, shaped me with broad shoulders and back muscles.

We stand almost forehead-to-forehead. An electric thread ignites right behind my eyes with a rage that rearranges my cells inside. It's fueled by seventeen years of rage and adrenaline. I power up to strike and aim my right fist for my mother's face. At the last minute, just as my knuckles almost graze her cheekbone, I divert my punch.

My hand punctures the sheetrock wall behind her. I can't remember what my mother does other than duck. I retract my arm from the hole in the wall and only see but can't feel my collapsed hand. From the nail of my baby finger down to my wrist, the outside half of my hand is folded into my palm. The anger, still in a blaze through me, blocks the pain, which comes soon after when my hand is a purple-black mangled mass because I don't go to the hospital.

After three days, my mother hands me her car keys. "Tell them you rough-housed with your brother."

Jonathan's off at college so it's a flat out untruth. I'd never known my mother to lie but I knew she'd skirt facts to protect the family image. She'd never want to admit my violence and let the world know we had problems. Big problems.

My swollen hand throbs on my lap all the way to the hospital. I'm frozen inside and don't feel a thing when the doctor re-breaks the bones before he can cast my hand because they've already set into a distorted form.

No pain, no more anger, nothing but frozen inside. I don't even feel lonely by myself in the hospital. Complete lockdown. When the head and heart lose their connection, this is all that's left. Lockdown: a sort of emotional suicide.

I thought everything would get better when I left home. Moving out would surely mean my life would change as every bit of rage dissolved into nothing but bliss. Grief would flutter away, joy would bounce right in front of me the minute I walked out the front door of my parents' house for good, my bags packed and ready for the good life. This was the first of several markers at which I thought everything would get better. When I move out, when I turn eighteen, when I have more money, when I have the right lover, when I get a house, get a car, move to this city, move to that city. What will make me feel better is always something outside of myself.

The first one, college, doesn't pan out. I head off to Ohio after high school for my first of several stints at college before I ever get my Bachelor of Arts degree. College is my only option because I don't have enough money to live on my own for long. I leave school after my first quarter, asked to leave after I round up a few other girls from the Black Student Union group to light fires in the dorm for white girls. I'd been asked to join the BSU, the catch-all group for anyone non-white, even though I couldn't identify my race. I instead graduated to the fast life in the streets back in Seattle.

The first time I load a spoon of dope, I go straight to the top of the class and cook up a speedball—heroin and coke. It's divine. The afternoon I first shoot up, I take a belt, cinch it around my bicep, pull the strap between my teeth, and give my vein a two-finger slap. I register—draw a little blood first before plunging. My palms sweat and my heart races, a horse inside pounding the track. The coke and heroin wave through me, a chemical orgasm, part birth and part death. It's all a gift, and I'm home!

I'm nineteen and run around with a boyfriend I've met at some party. Ron's a smooth-talking and soft-spoken Mexican American and just out of the joint. Now that I'm back from college in Ohio, Seattle's finally my city, not my family's. Jonathan is in Bloomington, Indiana, getting his MFA and is engaged. My father accepts an offer at Johns Hopkins University and my parents move to Baltimore. While my father goes more Ivy League, I dive further off the edge.

When I was at the tender age of eight, my father taught by example. We were on one of his sabbaticals. My brother and I learned how to smuggle. He drove our rented Fiat through Switzerland with Mother beside him and my brother and I in the back. As we crossed the border between Switzerland and France, Dad pulled over and stashed his banned Cuban cigars under my seat.

"Pretend you're sleeping," he said. In the car, we especially did what he demanded. We always had small foreign cars and his backhand swat reached all the way into our seats if something annoyed him.

Right away my adrenaline fizzed inside but I didn't know what it was. It's a feeling I'd grow addicted to, fear and excitement at the same time.

My brother and I slid down in our seats, closed our eyes, and flopped on one another. The border control waved Dad across the border, with his two "actor" kids sitting on top of his smuggled cargo.

A decade later, with three cocaine-filled balloons shoved into my vagina, I smuggle drug cargo across the border into Canada. I use my body as a vessel to smuggle drugs wherever and however I can, although my dad wouldn't have approved of my methods or cargo. I also carve out the inside of tampons and fill them with plastic-wrapped coke, then push as many as possible inside me to get the snow across the border.

If one of those balloons had popped or the plastic leaked in those tampons, I'd have absorbed enough coke to overdose in under a minute.

When George, boyfriend number four, winds up in the Monroe Correctional Complex about thirty miles outside of Seattle, we go into business. By now, drugs aren't a lifestyle, they're a living.

I stuff a drug-filled balloon in my mouth and walk into the visiting room with a pout and a swagger. I sit down with George and wink. A spark flickers in his eyes.

He leans towards me. I grab him by the back of the neck and spread his lips open with mine. My tongue thrusts the drug-filled balloon from my mouth to his. I walk out of there with the same swagger, proud of myself, relieved I'm not the one who has to swallow it and dig it out the other end.

We split the money from sales, one of the first times the entrepreneur comes alive in me. Risk and uncertainty, feelings I'm getting good at living with.

Chapter Ten

Act Normal

My regular setup for hauling dope works every time. With the top down and a trunk load of three suitcases stuffed full of weed and coke, I rip up the fast lane on Highway 101 out of San Diego in my convertible MG Midget. I'm headed towards Seattle. Two baby-blue suitcases with nine kilos of dope vacuum-sealed in shrink-wrap nestle below a false bottom in the trunk. The leather on the top suitcase is torn so I face it gouge-side down in the trunk, its raw ripped edges pressed against the dope inside worth thousands of dollars on the street.

One of my recent drug deals paid for this sweet machine with seventeen hundred dollars, all cash rubber-banded in stacks of twenty-dollar bills.

The speedometer clocks eighty miles an hour, James Brown rasps "I Feel Good" on my radio, and the rhythm of the ribbed road rocks underneath.

When Mother gifted me these Samsonite cases the year before for my high school graduation, she'd planned college essentials—new cords, sweaters, and toiletries—packed for Vassar or Radcliffe, not kilos of dope and cash crammed inside.

I veer around a bend. A roadblock ahead. The sight of khakis and two California Highway Patrolmen on the roadside sends my teeth into a clench, my jaw already clamped tight like a vise from too much coke in my veins. I'm ready, though. My decoy in back, a third bag, covers the bottom two in case cops stop me.

Inside my decoy bag, my clothes scrunch around three one-gallon plastic zip bags packed with cocaine. White crosses—AKA speed—fill another plastic bag. The third suitcase also shields my cargo in the event of rain. A blow-dry or slow heat at 100 degrees in the oven always cures damp cash. But who buys soggy weed? Well, me. Dry weed or perfume spilled-on weed, it doesn't matter. Weak opium or cheap hash, I don't care. Over-cut coke or pure-enough-to kill-you coke or heroin from the dirtiest dealer in town, I'll mainline anything.

Ahead, one CHP, his feet spread shoulder width, sweeps his arm in the air with a wide arc of "pull over." Even at a distance, he's the same lean tower of a man as my father, six-foot-four swimmer's build whose ready rage and alto boom of a voice sent me into a cower as a little girl.

A few car lengths away from The Man, instinct and adrenaline drive me into a panic of survival, a rush with my senses on high alert. Reality feels altered. It's the same high I got as a kid buried under my covers at night with my *Puffin Book of Poetry* and a flashlight.

The midday California heat beats down on my sun-darkened hands, one in a grip on the leather-covered steering wheel. My other hand yanks the stick to downshift and brake, the way my father taught me, like a racecar driver. The engine revs down from fourth gear into third, to second, then I accelerate and feel the power, the hug to the curve of the road.

I whiz by the first cop. When the second cop beckons with his hand, I swerve to the side of the road about twenty feet beyond the roadblock and glance in my rear-view mirror. The glare from both cops bounces out of the mirror while they saunter towards my car.

Uh oh, I say out loud to my steering wheel. The cops' measured approach towards my trunk turns into a swagger and the woozy wave from nerves in my stomach stirs even more. If only I could do a line or two of coke.

No time. Just sit.

The black leather seats cook inside the convertible and make me queasier, and even more since my black thick hair absorbs the sun and fries my scalp. A thin trail of sweat swizzles down my temples. Stay calm.

"Open your trunk," one of the cops says. My instinct jumps alive with adrenaline. I want to bolt. Something stops me. A suspicious half-smile curves on his lips. They might shoot me in the back if I run.

My trunk's packed with enough dope to get sent down for several consecutive life sentences. It's the late 1970s era of Rockefeller drug laws, and possession of two or more ounces of heroin, cocaine, or marijuana pulls the same penalty as second-degree murder.

Busted or not, no big deal. Sit tight.

The cop leans over my doorframe. I wish I'd tugged the top up earlier.

He scans the narrow space behind my seat. I smile. Nothing there. I keep my two-seater pristine. I'd stowed my ten-inch switchblade and .38 revolver underneath the carpet below my seat. A stack of maps in the back of my glove box conceals my kit—syringe, spoon, rubber strip to tie off, and a vial of water.

A Harley-Davidson revs around the bend. A middle-age woman straddles the machine, her shoulder-length hair pulled back into a ponytail. Loose strands flap in the wind, free.

Beads of sweat outline the tops of the cop's eyebrows. Before I step out of the car, I clench my eyelids tight as mini-fists to prepare for the worst, then open them and swing my legs out and plant my feet on the pavement. I stand firm in my uniform: flip-flops, jeans, and a long sleeved T-shirt to hide my track marks. His eyes dart up and down, from head to toe, and I turn away to let him size me up, my slight one hundred pounds dwarfed by his bulky frame dressed in khaki.

My rubber flip-flops smack my soles while I mosey in a Sunday stroll pace towards the rear of my car. One cop hovers on my left, centered behind the license plate. The other cop steps closer to my right side.

I bite the inside of my cheek, a ridge of scars there from so many years of gnaw gnaw gnaw in my mouth.

A hand motions towards my trunk. "Open up."

I turn my key in the lock. *Act normal.*

I have no idea what it means to act normal. What's normal for a girl like me born in prison, heroin-addicted at birth? What's normal for a Jewish family who adopts a multiracial girl, and parents who veil my race and conceal my prison birth? What's normal for a nineteen-year-old like me who runs drugs for a living, blueprints burglaries and bank scams, and who's the think tank in a small gang of ex-felons?

What's normal for anyone? How do we ever gauge if we're in the norm, or outside it? Somewhere along the way I learned to compare myself to others. Only it's a moving target. Every time I find someone or something "better" than I am, than I think I am, another "better" comes along. It's a sure way to never like myself, a lesson I'd learn only much later.

Pretend the lock's stuck. No. Say you need to pee. Nah, too obvious.

Run for it. Nope. Better not. My brain tangles in a debate.

Dread pulls my stomach muscles tighter. I force myself to keep my other hand from a dive into my jeans pocket to hide the bulge of the smooth film canister that presses into my thigh.

It's too obvious if I move my hand. Cocaine fills the plastic case; the snow I need to jolt my eyelids open on the long drive up the coast.

Dizzy from the heat and from the flood of adrenaline, I reconsider. Bolt! I calculate the risk and the steepness of the cactus-covered dusty incline to my right. I'd never make it up the hill.

My breath freezes in the bottom of my lungs.

"C'mon," the same cop says, "open it."

To my left, a sheer cliff plunges into the ocean.

Jump. Soar like you did as a kid, all those leaps out of a tree. But my hunger for thrill slips away when I envision multiple rounds pelted between my shoulder blades.

I flip open the trunk with one hand and dig the other into my pocket.

They'll never notice. I grip my fingers around the vial of coke buried in there.

"Just as I thought," the cop says.

I suck in a reservoir of air to fill my lungs. Maybe my last breath of freedom.

The cop repeats himself before I get a chance to realize the severity of my predicament.

"Just as I thought, but we gotta check anyway." The other slams my trunk closed, then they turn their backs to me. I draw my spine into a tight rod.

"Not enough room to fit anyone in there," one says.

What?

They'd completed their routine and random check for Mexicans smuggled into the U.S. inside trunks and under seats. They both step a few paces away from me to approach the next car, and I jump back into my car.

My lungs collapse with relief. "I'm free!" I say out loud.

My gut still tight, I shade my face like a visor to keep out what just happened. I jam my MG into first gear and hit the road, back on my warpath. Nothing slows me down. It's Deborah against the world.

Chapter Eleven

Gnawed

I reach for a glass of Jim Beam one day and stumble with a buckle-over pain in my gut. I try to straighten but can't. The pain rocks me to the floor until Ron, my current boyfriend, finds me. He half-carries me to his car and speeds to the hospital.

After the doctor prods and probes and ignores my moans, he shakes his head, and then schedules me for a barium test.

When I learn the test results, he says, "You have an advanced ulcer and it's developed over some years."

Some years? I'm only nineteen.

"That explains the bits of blood when I throw up," I tell him.

The doctor frowns, talks about stress, asks a thousand questions, and gives up, admonishing me when I fold up the paper he gives me with some list of special foods to eat. Bland food and no alcohol. Nothing about drugs.

Oh yeah, I have stress. My hair falls out in clumps and I've gnawed the inside of my cheek so much it aches from a ridge of scar tissue. I'm falling apart inside and out. But it doesn't make me quit drugs; my only friend, my family. Deep down I know I'll be better off if I stop. Next Friday, I promise myself. Or the week after. For sure by the end of the month.

The apprentice graduates the day one of the guys I run around with gives me a .38 Special with a mother-of-pearl inlaid grip. For the next five or so years, I spiral deeper into drugs and ratchet up my crimes.

My light brown skin and skinny body, down to the bones from too many drugs and not enough nutrition, lands me honest work. A giant of a woman approaches me on the street, places her hand on my arm. It chills me and I shrug it off.

"Would you be interested in modeling?" she says.

Me? Modeling? Since childhood, the messages in my head told me, *You're ugly.*

"I need some racial variety in my photo shoots."

I fidget and squirm in the studio. My looks, and this photographer focusing on them, make me feel awkward and embarrassed.

I model for a month and my daily $150 for a few hours of work ends up in the hands of drug dealers and in the cash registers of nightclubs and bars along the Seattle waterfront. Despite the regular money, I walk out on a photo shoot one afternoon and never go back—the same way I walk out on everything and everyone else, including my parents. My solution to everything: Stay on the move. No one can abandon me if I leave first.

Armed robbery, drug smuggling by the trunk load, stolen cash cards, and cash machine schemes fill my days until they lose their challenge. With no thrill to keep me, I switch to the big time. I enroll in bank teller training school for a two-week crash course. I devour every piece of information and receive straight-As. I have all the information I need to pull off an inside bank job with my guys.

Two days after the job, I retch and jerk like a rag doll. Dry heaves take over my body. I gag again and again until crimson phlegm springs from my mouth. I cling to the sides of the toilet bowl until my body finally gives up. I struggle to the bathroom mirror and stare. Blood vessels have burst in my eyes; I look as though I've used pink food coloring for eye drops. But by sunset, restless and still dizzy, I head back out on the street. I run into a woman I know from the bar, one of my drinking pals. We wander down University Way. What happens then changes my life.

Chapter Twelve

The End Before the Beginning

A scrawny white guy flirts with me as we're halfway down the boulevard, and when I can't divert his unwanted attention, the woman I've been drinking with flashes a four-inch buck knife and lurches toward the man. She plunges the blade into his stomach.

I turn around to get the hell out of there, but my feet have glued themselves to the asphalt. The guy clutches his bloody shirtfront, doubles over, and limps across the street. He disappears behind a building.

I never dreamed I'd be part of anyone getting hurt. My gun, my switchblade, they're only for swag. I didn't have it in me to actually use them on anyone.

I stand there, frozen. A sickness rises in my gut fused with terror at how derailed I've become. Terrified, I decide to ditch the bad life while I still have a life.

Even before I learn from a girlfriend about the local police and the FBI calling her to find me, I flee Seattle with my leather jacket, a few pairs of Levis, some t-shirts, my switchblade, and my pistol. I head for Minneapolis, praying my uncles and aunt will take me in.

Uncle Peretz, one of my mother's younger brothers and the one she's closest to, takes me in until I get on my feet in Minneapolis. He's single, in his 60s, and still sees me as his "Little Debbie." But now I'm even littler. He last saw me built when I trained as a swimmer teen athlete. By the time I arrive on the run from the cops, he doesn't let on how I've changed: barebones and fragile, inside and out. My parents, relieved to hear I've surfaced, call me, not so happy, on the night I arrive in Minneapolis. Dad bellows through the phone.

"The FBI is looking for you."

I shrug at the phone. "Yeah, I know."

"Now you'll never get a job!"

My dad slams the receiver and I don't care. Who needs a job? I need dope.

My uncle hires a lawyer for the investigation of my crimes in Seattle. His kindness warms my heart and hurts at the same time. Weeks and weeks pass and somehow they never charge or arrest me. I spend those months white-knuckling my way off of drugs. The tremors and cold sweats envelop my body. I fight back by heavy drinking with my uncle. He hits the bar every night with his friends, and I join him to get the alcohol in me.

I move into my own apartment after a year of living with my uncle. My parents and I protect our fresh start and never discuss my dark years or my childhood. We never speak about where I went after quitting college or what I did. But they do have a lot to say about my drinking.

Drug-free, and even though my bouncy brain still fights me, I return to college work, still restless inside, still a rebel. I keep far from my parents' field, literature, and instead graduate with a degree in economics. Not the best reason to choose a course of study, just to rebel against parents. But I did, and also because Karl Marx and the study of economy and social justice interested me. How could they not with the influences of 1960s and Power to the People so strong in my childhood.

A degree doesn't mean I know how to settle down, though. Just because I take action to live in a more traditional lifestyle doesn't mean I know how to settle all the unrest in my spirit. My outside and inside don't match. I'm still a mess inside, still confused, living with questions about where I'm from, what race I am.

I get the notion if I stay on the move and fill my memory bank with new ones, there won't be any room for old memories.

Fact versus memory.

If I keep on the move, maybe I can remake facts by making new memories to push the old ones out. It takes me forever to understand I hated the facts of my beginnings, not the memories.

I float through a series of short-term jobs: I staff a group home for court-adjudicated girls, model for print shots occasionally, work for the county to organize a meals-on-wheels program for seniors.

Along with the drugs, I also quit my criminal ways, everything cold turkey, more from fear and boredom than from anything else. As the saying goes, I was sick and tired of being sick and tired.

With my pool-shooting and party talents, I can't resist the Minneapolis nightlife and clubs. I miss the high-action drug adrenaline so much I hook up with a hard-partying crowd of theater people and dancers. I dive into a series of romances and reckless sex with both men and women. Some turn into relationships for a few months, maybe a year or two, but nothing longer. Why would they? I don't know how. I never let myself join my family growing up, so committing to a relationship is next to impossible.

My first passion, dance, shoots to the surface as soon as I clean up. I train again and pick up where I'd left off in my childhood classes. No tutu this time. Instead, my athletic nature and small build are perfect for modern dance. At last I make my first serious career choice since drug running: I train to audition for a dance company. I've never before held a dream for myself other than to find out where I'd come from. The dream takes me to London for a long summer of dance training and the thrill of attending every theater and dance performance where I can find a cheap ticket. I live in a spare bedroom in my parents' flat, my father there for another Sabbatical year to work on one of his books.

Back in Minneapolis after the summer, excitement and nerves bubble in my stomach for a week. One day in class before an audition I dislocate my knee and end up in a cast from crotch to ankle. My first night home from the hospital, I ask a friend to bring me a bottle of Johnny Walker Red. Booze and cocaine help squash the physical pain and drown my despair about losing my dream. Ten months imprisoned in a cast and once again, I'm an addict.

It takes a certain kind of stamina to chase a dream, and it takes even more to accept when the dream crashes. I didn't have it in me to face the crash.

Chapter Thirteen

A White Knuckle Ride

A year later, at a house party with cases of empty champagne bottles strewn about and the glass coffee table covered with coke, a handful of women and I dare one another. We make a deal to get chemical dependency tests. No one else follows through but me. The intake test at the outpatient Hazelden Women's Clinic produces disturbing results. The chemical dependency counselor gestures for me to sit in the plastic chair beside hers.

"Deborah, you need to get into treatment soon as possible."

I lean back, shake my head.

"You're wrong."

I sling my bag over my shoulder and flounce out of there. Over the next month I traipse around town for tests at five other agencies. The woman at the second agency helps me feel safe with her gentle smile. I like her until she speaks.

"You need treatment, Deborah. Immediately."

I storm out of her office and do the same for counselors at the next three agencies, all of whom seem obsessed with treatment. Tendrils of panic and hopelessness try to latch onto my brain but I shake them out of my head. I don't need treatment. I don't need anybody.

I'll quit on my own.

So I do. I take myself to hell.

This time, a white-knuckle ride with no straps and no thrills, cold turkey gets me one hundred percent horror. Day one, my body drains of strength. Same in days two and three, and the cold sweats ruin not only my sheets but also the mattress. I shake so bad, I struggle to turn over the mattress to get the soaked side down so I can sleep on dry sheets. On and on for days—cold sweats, nausea, and sometimes in a hot dizzy confusion. I can't tell if it's the alcohol, the coke, the Quaaludes a friend gives me, or the mushrooms another friend brings over to smoke with me. Week two, I continue to retch, my body exhausted from my stomach's repairing.

After weeks of white knuckling it, I take one last slam of Johnny Walker Red. It throws me into more tremors. I kneel in the bathroom, bent over the toilet, and long for Mother. The memory of her wiping my bangs from my fever-hot forehead, holding a damp cool washcloth against her little girl's face, nearly tear me apart. Mother. I hadn't ever thought about her tenderness before.

I survive the weeks of cold turkey. Bags of hard candy and chewing gum help, the sugar craving so intense I often spend ten dollars a day on hard candy.

I make it. Clean. I stay that way for a year. But then I go to a party. I enter to thumping music and glance left. The guests fade from my sight as I stare at the gorgeous white mountain of coke on the coffee table. The vision yanks me by the solar plexus and drags me over, every nerve on alert. A pile of coke—free for all guests. A little voice warns me from some part of my brain but I wave it away. My body wants that coke.

By the end of the month, I'm on cocaine drug runs between Minneapolis and New York every other weekend with my roommate, Pat. But on my fifth trip something goes wrong.

On a midnight run to get a corned beef sandwich somewhere near Times Square, my throat starts to close. My dope has been cut with something bad. I clutch my neck, struggle to breathe.

Pat grabs me by the arms, then releases me.

"Damn, damn," she says.

She flags a cab. The cabbie grips the steering wheel so tight he has two-tone knuckles. When he presses his foot to the floor, my head shoots back against the headrest. He screeches alongside a drugstore and Pat springs from the car, then pulls me out. I grab at snippets of air. Fear pumps through my blood. I'll die in the street.

I hear someone screaming at me. Pat. She throws a box of Benadryl into my lap, opens the packet inside, clutches my mouth between her thumb and forefinger, and throws one capsule down my throat. I have no room to swallow. I fight. She cocks my neck back, seals my lips so I have to swallow. I choke on the first gel cap, but manage to swallow the second one on my own. My air passages reopen.

Tears stream down my face. I could have died—right on the street. I shake, rub my arms.

"I can't do this anymore."

"Sure you can," Pat says. "You just had a bad hit."

She glances at me, the residue of panic flickering in her eyes.

Fear strikes me when I'm back home in Minneapolis two days later. I know I need help. Something clicks. I grab the phone, call a chemical dependency counselor, and arrange a session with her. I listen more than talk and reply to her intake questions with bare-bones answers. While I'm not conscious of this, the therapist suggests my behavior and escapades were my way to return to where I first felt loved—in prison. I'd been taunting the world to put me back where I'd first known love.

She goes on to explain that what others had considered my bravado as a girl had been related more to a lack of impulse control, possibly a problem extended longer because of developmental delays as an infant.

Then it starts to stand out in the light: After I read the letter and grew conscious about my birth in prison, my life had distorted forever. And I'd failed to understand how desperate I'd been to prove my love for the mother I'd lost, my loyalty lodged deep inside me. *No other mother will get my love*, the little girl of me had vowed. Not only this, but the more I thought I could emulate her, the more I'd be just like her. Closer and closer. *They could separate me from her but I'll never leave her. Never. Ever. I'll love her forever and ever.*

No wonder I'd never let Mother get close to me, both physically and in my heart. She didn't stand a chance with my fierce loyalty. No one did. She was the only mother with the stamina to wait for me.

From the moment I read the letter I'd become obsessed about my roots, as much about my birthplace as the woman who'd birthed me. I needed to know more, feel more, see more. Know everything.

As much as I'd tried to lock up my prison birth secret, it had leaked out its poison as secrecy does. All the love from my parents couldn't remove the stigma I felt, especially because keeping my past a secret had added to the shame.

"You've stunted your emotional development," the therapist tells me.

"What do you mean 'stunted'?"

"You're two decades behind."

"What?" The word springs out. I take a deep breath. "So what can I do about it?"

She shakes her head.

"Starting drugs so young, using for the next twenty years. There's no guarantee you'll catch up."

Catch up what? I stagger home, shaking inside and out. Despair dulls my vision. A driver in a Mercury honks me out of my daze and from almost denting the hood of his car. He yells out of his window.

"You shouldn't be on the road!"

I agree. I'm not old enough. Without drugs, I'm back at twelve, back where I left off before I started using. Twelve! A thirty-two-year-old body with a twelve-year-old inside. At least that explains why I'm a perfect match for my nineteen-year-old boyfriend, a guy I met at a dance club.

At home, I curl onto the sofa and hug my knees. Mother and friends call during the weeks after. I fight not to cry all the time when I answer the phone. Terror clutches at my throat when I have to talk. Terrified of who I am and at the same time not knowing who I am.

I can't go out. How can I face the outside world?

Chapter Fourteen

Another Secret

Chip, chip, chip. That's how I break through the walls I've built, my fortress around me. Each chip feels like a slab of concrete crashing to the ground. But when I'm clean and sober, fear opens into a raw wound. A smidgen of a crevice opens to allow my parents in. I take baby steps in a giant's shoes to close the gap and reacquaint myself with them.

Mother invites me for lunch at their home in Champaign, Illinois, where my dad teaches at the university. She, Dad, and I sit at the table and Mother serves noodles and butter, my all-time favorite since I was little.

I look from my mother to my father, then back to my mother and feel the volcano erupt in my stomach, the familiar rubber band ball about to explode. It shoots up to my lungs. I fight to keep the words in. They burn at my throat. Mother and Dad raise their forks. I've held it in so long, now I have to say it, not ask, just blurt it out.

"I know I was born in prison."

Both their forks stop in midair. They look from me, to each other, and back to me.

"But . . . how?"

I don't answer.

"Why didn't you tell me?"

Mother's shoulders sag.

"We worried what would happen if you found out."

I almost laugh into my pasta. Yeah, this way worked out so much better.

Mother manages a smile and a heaviness lifts from me. We say no more. I have an answer at least. They meant well but didn't know any better. These days, more resources are available for families with transracial adoption. I blamed my parents for what they didn't know, their lack of information and resources.

Mother comes back with me to stay a few days in Minneapolis. We museum-hop the first day. After lunch at the Art Institute, we charge up the granite stairs to the museum's top floor and stand transfixed by the Veiled Lady, a marble sculpture from the 1800s. We both love her crisp marble features and white veil sculpted in the illusion of gauzy, transparent silk to cover her face. Mother reaches for my hand and my breath catches.

My habit has always been to pull away. But I've kicked other habits. I slow my breathing, let my palm rest against hers. Still twelve inside, still cautious, but a new twelve. We hold hands, the first I remember where I let my palm melt into hers. I'm thirty-something and just hired my mother. Some adoptions take a while to work. Some don't work at all, but since I've grown to understand, there's no blame in my story. I've also come to believe some things just take time. Decades, sometimes. I've never met another person with the stamina my mother had.

Each time Mother visits, we visit the Veiled Lady and the tightness inside me begins to thaw. When I visit Mother in Illinois, we swim laps in my parents' backyard pool and play piano together.

I remain cautious around Dad even though he's stopped his backhand swats. His intense intellectual energy and outbreaks of rage still frighten me. Just his presence in the room has me retreating into my shell.

But Mother, my sweet mother, white-haired and wrinkled and now seventy-four, her eyes glow, her heart pours out to me. She's waited so long for the daughter she's always wanted. I open up and receive and return that precious love. At last, I have a mama. At last I'm a daughter to the woman who believed in me even when I didn't believe in myself.

No longer in a fight against myself, the world, my family, I allow my love of writing poetry and short stories to reignite. I couldn't stop writing if I wanted to. My parents delight with me in the celebration when I win the American Association of University Women Poetry Award. Soon after my poetry prize, I'm awarded a series of grants and short story awards. From this, I take on my first full-time job, a freelance writer-in-residence in public schools.

Despite my bond with Mother, part of me still craves my prison mom, to know more about her. I call a search agency to locate her.

"I'm pretty confident we'll find her for you," the "search angel" says.

My heart somersaults. Would I look like her? What would she think of me? My mind ping-pongs questions for weeks, sending me from excitement to fear and back again. The agency calls a month later.

"We have news for you."

My breath catches in my throat. The hairs on my skin spring up like miniature soldiers. Okay, breathe. I've waited forever to get this far, to get this close.

"I'm afraid your mother is dead."

I roll the letters around over and over. Dead. The word taunts me. All these years, so much chaos and lost time, so much brokenness and yearning . . . and she's dead.

"Deborah, are you okay?"

I nod into the phone.

"You have a half-brother."

A brother. A link to my birth mom.

"I've got his phone number. Have a pen?"

I scramble for a pen, drop it, and grab it again.

I hang up and stare at my brother's phone number. She's dead. So is my life-long dream to meet her. I yearn for a needle in my arm to kill the fear, the sorrow. A slam down of Johnny Walker Red, anything. It takes everything in me not to get high.

Instead, I exhale, pick up the receiver, and dial. Nick picks up on the second ring. Before I know it, I'm on a flight back to Seattle to meet my family. Besides Nick, who's about ten years older, in his late forties, I'm met with open arms by aunts, uncles, and cousins, all of whom live in the Seattle area. They welcome me as though I've just returned from a long summer away at camp.

Nick and I had different fathers. Talk about shocked. He thought he was an only child. Our mother never told him he had a sister, never told him she was pregnant when she was sentenced. She'd been in and out of prisons, jails, and reform school since she was a teen, most sentences drug related, as is the case today where 85 percent of all incarceration for both women and men relate to drugs in one way or another. A good case for treatment, rehab, and education as one solution to incarceration.

One of our aunts raised Nick, and he was used to our mother going off to prison. I'd later find out about her multiple sentences in several prisons around the country, most crimes related to her heroin addiction.

Secret on secret. This time I'm the family secret.

I don't know how much time he spent with her, but

it was enough for him to recognize her in me. Within moments of our embrace, Nick says, "Your voice, your gestures, you move your head like our mother." A thrill shoots through my solar plexus. I beam, delighted to be part of her. Nick leads me into the house and perches next to me on the sofa. He reaches for an album and places it on my lap.

"Our mom's photo album."

My stomach flips.

"Her brother, our Uncle Tom, kept it hidden from me until you called." Tears brim in his eyes. I blink back my own. He reaches over and opens the album. The first page makes me gasp. I stare at a baby picture of me and a lock of my hair. My mother kept a lock of my hair. I stroke it with my forefinger and swear I feel her love seep into me. It takes a while before I can turn that page.

I move on to photos of her. A sense of belonging fills my being. I could dive into those photos and live inside them with her. One more puzzle piece slides into place—I have her hands, her smile, the fire in her black eyes. At last I see I look like someone else. But I have differences too, with my eyes more almond shaped, my nose smaller, darker coloring, other things that keep me wondering what am I? What about the other half of me? She's Greek, I learn, and I'm so much more. But what?

Someone knocks on the door and my brother comes back with an olive-skinned sixty-something woman about my height.

"This is our cousin, Sophie."

Excitement bursts into hugs and smiles and more family, more connections with Martha, my prison mom, or Margo, as I learn she liked to be called.

"I needed to see you," she says, "tell you something your mom had planned."

She smiles.

"Something your mother yearned to do her whole life."

She looks from me to my brother and back to me. I want to shake every bit of information out of her, my core desperate to know everything.

"Right before she died, your mother stood at the nursery window in the hospital looking at the babies. She planned to hire a detective to find you as soon as she got better."

My mother had throat cancer and expected she'd heal and get out of the hospital.

The thought of her at the nursery window with her hope of finding me makes me feel as though I might topple over, dizzy from sadness. Grief strikes my heart and sadness engulfs me. It wasn't just me, one-sided. She'd yearned to meet me and we'd missed each other. I can barely stand the crack in my heart.

Another cousin arrives, Madlyn, dark-haired and lean as I. She sits with me and clasps my hand in both of hers.

"You know she named you Madlyn Mary, a family name."

"Madlyn Mary." I run the sounds over my tongue, imagine our twelve months together in prison, her whispering my name. But then an image of Mother springs into my mind. I laugh.

"My adoptive parents are Jewish," I say. "Madlyn Mary, not exactly a Jewish girl's name."

It's a whirlwind of a weekend. I return to Minneapolis with more than memories and stories from my new family. They've given me a silk scarf of hers, a diamond ring, and an engraved wooden cross, all nested in my jewelery box to this day. The walls I'd constructed around myself begin to crumble. A last patch of wholeness fills me after meeting my family. I have something I need to do. I go into my bedroom and drag my suitcase from the back of my closet. I open it and pull out my pistol. I run my fingers over the barrel. I haven't used it up to now except to threaten people in a few heists, over a decade ago. Time to let go of my past even more.

Its weight in my hands haunts me. What would have happened if I'd continued on my old path, my life of crime, drugs, and self-destruction?

I check the chamber: frozen. I rise to my feet, stride out to the dumpster, and toss it inside. A piece of my dark past I'm glad to throw away.

Chapter Fifteen

Mother and Daughter, At Last

Something's still raw in me like I'm an over-ripe raspberry balanced on a single-edge razor blade. It gets sliced no matter which way it rolls, and that's me, shaky and raw, my insides scrambled and carved up but I don't know why.

After all, I'm clean. I've straightened up. I've even begun to work out, using my body to rewire my brain. Most days I'm in the gym for a few hours, working my way into better and better health.

Still something claws at me. I've finally connected with my family, above all, my mother. I've met my birth family. I know a little more about my birth mom, and still, I need more. Two questions haunt me.

What am I? What race or races? I'm sick of checking the Other box. Sick of telling people I don't know. Wherever I go, people think I'm one of them. I'm sick of this, too. By fitting in too many places, I fit nowhere.

And then there's the prison. How is it really possible anyone is born in prison? I've never met anyone with a story like mine, and even though I've grown to accept it as fact, sometimes it still doesn't feel real.

I try to push my questions away but the isolation floods me. I bury it with work. Always an entrepreneur, an idea person, I continue a freelance life and as a contract writer-in-residence in public schools across the state of Minnesota. I have a million ideas and a mountain of energy to burn now that I'm back to my true creative nature. I write a book of daily meditations for the drug and alcohol recovery market, targeted for multiracial and multicultural readers. Fairview Press publishes the book and it sells well enough to launch me into several other creative and entrepreneurial enterprises. Since the book's now out of print I'm in the process of re-writing it for a new release. I also dabble in real estate investment and buy and sell a few commercial properties.

The risk and adventure I loved from running the streets shows up in my entrepreneurial work. It takes risk to shape an idea and implement it into a business, the same risk I knew in the streets. It takes guts and courage to believe in your ideas and bring them out into the world. I'm best at the idea part and not the best at the business end of things.

I plow the most energy into reconnecting with Mother. Then one day she calls. Frantic, she asks, "Can you meet me at the Mayo Clinic?"

"What? What's going on?"

"I've been diagnosed with . . ."

The pause grips around my lungs and cuts off my breath.

I hear her breath catch.

"I've got ovarian cancer."

"Oh, Mother."

I stumble backward and somehow manage to stop the phone before it slips from my hand. It can't be. Mother never gets sick. A strong, healthy seventy-something woman, she swims laps, gardens, snowshoes, works out in aerobics classes every week.

She and my father drive from Chicago and I rush to meet her at Mayo, about an hour south of Minneapolis.

While doctors explore whether her cancer is advanced or not, I stay with her for three weeks in the hotel, weeks both desolate and precious, which give us both a gift: time together and the intimacy to grow closer. We have two decades to make up—all the years of my childhood where I pushed her away.

I sit at her side by her hospital bed and hold her hand, stroke her pale skin. She turns to me and smiles.

"You know, we wanted to adopt more children, at least a third child, but you were so troubled and difficult, we couldn't handle more."

Do I really need to know what I prevented in her dream, her vision for a family of three kids? Then my heart swells—she's shared this secret with me, trusts me even after all those years of broken trust. But soon it shrivels in shame. What else have I caused? What else have I prevented her from achieving in her life?

Week seven and Mother heads back to Illinois to begin chemo. I call her two or three times every day. Month after month after month I fly in to visit, bring her fluffy socks, bathrobes, magazines, all I can to comfort her. But I know what brings the most comfort by the glisten in her eye, the smile on her full lips: Her daughter sits at her side.

She's waited these thirty years for her daughter. A mother's bond can hold incredible love and stamina, even if not a link by birth. At last we both embrace the bond. Saddest of all, it's toward the end of her life.

— Chapter Sixteen —

Weeping Mother

I'm a believer in things happening for a reason, even if the reason is obscure or painful. After twenty years of my written requests to the prison for more information, the gates open with a welcome for a private tour. My mother's on her deathbed, and Warden Atwood calls to invite me to visit Alderson. The timing couldn't have been worse.

Prison is my birth country. I yearn to visit the way adopted persons from Korea, India, China, the Philippines, South America, Romania, Russia, and every other country abroad yearn to visit their own homelands. Most people at least hold a curiosity about their roots. Even non-adopted people seek their homelands.

I'm going home, home to prison.

Even though I've been raised in middle-class privilege,

I've felt exiled and paralyzed, deprived of my homeland. At last I'm headed there, a place I've only imagined and most often doesn't seem real. How can anyone be born in prison?

The gates of a new threshold open where I'm about to replace the impressions of prison promoted by television, movies, and public opinion with my own personal and private images. I'm about to enter what I've imagined as my nest, my one and only place of comfort.

It's 1990. I've exchanged a trunk load of dope for a B.A. in economics, a clean record, and in my garage, two collector Vespa scooters alongside a classic MG, but not the same one from my drug runs on Highway 101. Legitimate money from several businesses I've founded fills my bank account, although not often with much to spare.

Alderson nestles in the Appalachian Mountains. Muddy Creek and Wolf Creek run nearby, streams named as if characters in my life story. Morning mists cover the prison each dawn with a shroud of fog. Hummingbirds dart through willows and hover above fields of lobelia.

Mother would attract hummingbirds to our garden in Seattle with tubes of honey outside the kitchen window.

"Legends link this little bird to a miracle," she told me, "the miracle of joyful living from life's difficult circumstances."

It took me thirty years to understand the legends of the hummingbird. Instead of relishing miracles, I felt cursed. I carried a mantra around in my head and repeated it over and over: No one's born in a prison. Nobody.

The curse fueled my anger and my insecurity. A defective adopted multiracial girl born to a heroin addict in prison. My self-esteem sat somewhere in here: I might as well be dumped from a sky-high crane into a vat of acid and tar.

The night before my prison tour I stay a mile away from the prison. I check in to Riverview Motel, its address, Rural Route 2 Box 0. When I pull up, my headlights hit the motel sign: We Hardly Exist. Exactly how I've felt most of my life, a Big Zero, invisible scum of the earth, a speck of dirt.

The Riverview connects to the town gas station, which shares a wall with the grocery store, the store's shelves lined with cans of Spam, big jars of pickles, pink eggs in a jar, pickled pigs feet and snouts, sardines, potted meat, and Yoo-hoo chocolate soda. Not quite the gourmet grocery stores and delis in Seattle where Mother used to fill her shopping basket with capers, pure olive oil, and Bibb lettuce.

I approach the gates of the Alderson Federal Women's Prison in West Virginia with a wobble in my legs. Two federal officers dressed in dark blue uniforms stand on the other side of the gate and eye me through the wrought-iron bars.

I hand over my papers to the shorter officer. She nods to her colleague and the gate opens. I wonder if they've kept my earlier paperwork, the letters I've written year after year. Each time I'd appeal for facts about my birth, for details about my prison mom. Always I'd close my letters with one question: Can you tell me what race I am?

"This way."

She flanks me to the main prison building, a red brick two-story rectangle. Is this what it looked like when they transferred my mom here? Her sentence began in the Medical Center in Lexington, Kentucky, once called the U.S. Narcotics Farm where addicts and psychiatric inmates were sent for the "Lexington Cure." They moved her to Alderson when they learned she was pregnant.

Footsteps crunch behind me. I shoot a glance over my shoulder. The tall officer follows us a few paces behind.

A horn blast pierces the compound. I jump and the officer says, "Three o'clock inmate count." The inmates race to their cottages.

I'm back where I belong.

The officers escort me to the administration building across the compound. Six two-story brick colonial buildings sprawl around the campus-like prison in a semi-circle.

An inmate sweeps the entry. I follow her movements, mesmerized.

Did my mom stand here on these steps once, hunched over a broom? Or did they relieve her of any work duty? She'd arrived five months' pregnant with me.

Lost in my thoughts, I stumble up the stairs and knock into an officer. Inside, another inmate swabs the faded tile floor like a sailor in a t-shirt with an inked inmate number and a string mop.

We reach the control center and the guard stops.

"Wait here."

I nod, my feet glued to the worn tile. Three officers surround me. The buzz of foot traffic casts a trance on me.

A line-up of five administrators slide their clip-on plastic badges into a steel cradle embedded in a steel ledge framed by a bubble of bulletproof glass around the control room. Inside, three guards monitor moments of freedom and inspect name-stamped aluminum tokens in exchange for badges, keys, memos, radios, and authority.

Two correction officers break the spell with their laughter at an inside joke.

Five minutes of waiting turn into twenty. For all the admin staff here, no one's around to process me through security.

At last an officer waves me into a room. Inside, behind a metal desk, another officer tilts back on his chair and gestures for me to sit opposite him. He pushes a stack of forms across the desk.

"Fill these in."

I finish the forms just when a female officer bursts into the room.

"Prints," she says. She gestures with her head towards the door. I shove the stack of papers back across the desk and follow her. Down the hall a different officer presses and rolls my fingertips onto a black ink cushion.

So this is what my mom went through.

"We need two sets," the officer says, "one for the FBI, one for the BOP."

"Doesn't the Bureau of Prisons have enough on file about me?" I ask.

She ignores my question. "Other hand."

I scrub in the sink with their grease remover but a faded shadow of ink still embeds in my fingertips. I lick my thumbs and rub over the other fingers but the stains don't lift.

"This way," the officer says. She opens the front door, the grass compound on the other side. On the way out I fight to return the guards' generous smiles and instead wave my hand like a schoolgirl.

My heart skips a beat. At last. I'm back.

I'm here, at long last inside what's obsessed me for a lifetime, where I've been secretly in love with even the word itself, prison, and every word related to my first home. As a girl I'd imagined them all: a dungeon, lock-up, the joint, the pen, a penal institution, reformatory, detention center, the can, slammer, clink.

My feet march on the prison compound: left, right, left, right. I can't believe I'm here, the same prison where my mom spent ten years, where she started out her sentence pregnant and a long-time heroin addict, where I lived for one year, born with her addiction. I screamed the place down 24/7, spat out milk because my body craved the drug it'd grown with, and was plagued by vomiting and diarrhea, which is common for heroin-exposed babies. At six months, I still couldn't take in my mom's milk, so the prison nurse concocted a molasses formula.

Only half of babies exposed to heroin are born alive, and those who survive need expert care to deal with the withdrawal and related developmental delays. Ten percent of heroin infants have chromosome changes, and six percent are born with neurological damage.

Why did Lady Luck grant me life? Or was this my fate, my destiny to not only survive my birth but also return here? Was it more than luck?

Since every drug passes from a mother's bloodstream through the placenta to the fetus, drug addiction in the mothers causes addiction for the baby. Since the drug's no longer available after birth, the baby's central nervous system becomes over stimulated and causes withdrawal symptoms, which can last for two to six months. Findings suggest chronic intrauterine exposure to heroin may cause hyperactivity, brief attention span, and delayed cognitive, perceptive, and motor skills, and other developmental delays. Babies who suffer from heroin withdrawal also struggle with eating difficulties, over-stimulation, and irritability. They're difficult to console or comfort. If only my parents had been given the resources and education to better understand this, and also been informed about how to raise a non-white child in a white community, our relationship and my childhood could have been so much easier. But I'm not much of an "If only . . ." person. I take the past as it is and reframe it to give me a perspective through a new lens.

Like a dandelion puff in a flutter from a breeze, I fly off above the prison in a distortion of time and space, my cells in a dance. Did my mom feel mind flips like this, too? I'm at a threshold I've imagined my whole life. I fight going into emotional lockdown, my default for everything new when I don't know where it fits inside.

"Let's begin on the compound," the officer says and launches into an impromptu history of the prison. "Our most famous inmates include Billie Holiday, Tokyo Rose, Squeaky Fromme," she adds. Martha Stewart would come later. How ironic she and my prison mom share the same first name.

No metal fences surround the camp, other than the one-hundred-acre rural span outside the prison, a natural barrier of rolling West Virginia hills.

Come back. I need to rein in my focus. Time and place converge in one plane. I can't ground my body in the present. Come back. I want—need—to savor my return home, remember every second of what took me a lifetime to find.

"Are you okay?" the officer asks.

I press my eyelids together, desperate to shake it off and keep this weirdness to myself.

But the time distortion wins. We're now in an empty basement room in another building the size of the Riverview Gas-n-Stop. A déjà vu of this room flashes through me along with a dizzy spell. About to pass out, I press the palm of my hand against the door to brace myself.

Faded green paint chips fall to the ground from the pressure of my hand. "This paint," the officer says, "the same since your birth here, never painted, same since the prison first opened."

"This is where we once released sheets of paper for

letters and envelopes to prisoners. Your mom probably carried you in here every day."

I hang on to her words, inhale this prison air, this landscape I'd shared with my mom. A year of perfection I'd created in my mind.

My breath races faster. Don't let her see. I try to hide the heave of my shoulders so the officer won't notice them rise and fall. I'm not ready to let anyone into my feelings yet, especially a stranger, an authority figure. Fast-paced everything: heart, breath, vision, like a trapped animal set free.

"Up there," the officer points to the ceiling, its faded white paint now speckled in chips. "The chapel. Service every Wednesday and Sunday. You probably attended church with your mom. They baptized you here, I'm sure."

Baptized? I'm raised in a Jewish family and I'm baptized!

Jewish mysticism speaks about two powerful muscles in the brain: memory and imagination. But what about the pocket in between, where memory reaches out to imagination but can't quite connect? All my life I stored my prison birth secret in this pocket to hide it from myself and from the world.

My mind pitches me into this brain space in this dank chipped-paint basement beneath the prison chapel. With silence all around except in my head, I'm transplanted back in time into a Baptist service and the reverb of a chapel full of women. Hands clap, women sing spirituals, feet stomp. I'm desperate to know if this is my imagination or a memory reawakened.

We walk the compound again towards another corner of the prison.

Then something doesn't fit. What about all those times she was sent to isolation? She couldn't have kept me in the hole. Where was I, and who took care of me in those weeks on many occasions when she went to isolation?

When I ask the officer, she answers a quick reply like I've just inquired about the time of day.

"Oh, you went to the Hole with her."

Just when I begin to wrap my hands around the deeper truth of my prison birth, I'm learning I spent time in the hole with my prison mom. I have so many questions where I'll never know the answers. What on earth does a baby do in the Hole for week after week? Isolated within four walls, no sensory stimulation, what does a baby do in the

Hole? What does anyone do but go mad? Me, I had my prison mom. How bad can that be?

Once again, I force myself to lean into unanswered questions and things I can't reconcile. I use my newfound discipline to do this and not let the uncertainty eat me up.

Grass and concrete layer the compound but the ground has fallen away in this out-of-body drift. My feet float, air-filled dumplings. Another space jump. I appear on the first floor of another two-story brick colonial, this one deserted. The afternoon sun slants through an open door into the hallway. When we enter, the officer says, "Your mother delivered you in here."

My head's about to explode from emotional overload and from the humid 95-degree West Virginia August heat. I can't speak to the officer. I've lived with my prison roots a secret for so many decades; when I finally stand here in the place of answers, I'm still silent, mute the way I was for long periods at a time as a little girl.

My senses spring into a primal dance, my body drenched in sweat. I imagine backwards. I sense the air vibrate with the angst of my mom in delivery, her uncertainty about the future of her baby. I tweak my cotton shirt at the collar to lift and unglue my shirt off my back.

The officer's shoes scuff on the tile and echoes across the empty hospital room. I jump. She looks at me, waits for questions. Was it a difficult birth? Did my mom pant hard for air? Part of me, desperate to ask, tries to speak but another part inhales a long draw. I'm speechless. I suck in the scent of my mom's birth sweat from thirty years ago.

Another time distortion sweeps me up. Our collective thump comes alive again in this hospital room we shared. It wipes out the panic, the anxiety I've carried with me for a lifetime. Joy floods through me and I blink back the tears. No way I want this officer to see me cry.

We inch across the compound. The officer leads me into Cottage C, two floors of long rows of rooms on either side of the hall. I try to say something, anything. But my throat locks. I transport back into my pre-verbal first year here. Only my senses fire, my cells alive without words.

She points towards an open door on my left at the end of the first floor hall. I fight my out-of-body instinct. For a second, I have no idea how or why we approach this door, number seven. Then it smacks me in the solar plexus.

The cell I shared with my mom.

The officer and floor guards hang back. I approach the door. My breath catches. Air traps in a cave at the bottom of my lungs.

The last place my mom held me. She loved me in this room. I loved her here.

I imagine her rage and helplessness about me as I'm taken from her. For the first time I think of her pain and loss, not just mine.

I try to step into the room but I can't lift a foot. I lean forward, bent at my waist to scan the room for a second. I turn back into the hall and press my back against the wall. I can't breathe, my head about to explode again.

I turn again, try to enter that five-by-eight-foot room, my first home. There's just enough space for a table, chair, and bed to fit. I stand in the doorway and the cell soothes me, like a scene in my dollhouse I played with as a girl.

My home, this cell. I slept in here, ate, crawled around, and now I'm back. My body melts, relaxes into a comfort like nowhere else before.

Go in, get in there.

My skin starts to itch, panic stirs in my gut. Go!

I shake my head. I can't.

I blank out then soar back to age one, in the middle of the night when someone snatched me from my mom's bed and flew me to Seattle. I learn later it's a Federal Marshall who flew with me from West Virginia to Seattle and into the hands of my first foster family.

Part of me yearns to dive onto the coarse tungsten-colored blanket, bury my face in the bed, and cry.

But it never happens. Now, I wish I had.

Some people shoot heroin, others overdose on shame, guilt, and secrets. I'd lost myself in all of it. I'd hoped going back to my first home would be a tonic in my healing and forgiveness.

Before I drive away from the prison that day in my rental car, I stand in the parking lot and turn to face my first secret—prison. I've faced my biggest stigma, but I still didn't want to share it with the world. I hadn't told my family about my visit to the prison, and just a handful of friends know about the trip.

All that changes three months later when a radio producer calls and leaves me a voice mail.

Chapter Seventeen

Full Circle

"Deborah, we'd like to interview you inside your birthplace, in your birthmom's prison," a producer from Public Radio says in her voice mail.

It's my prison, too.

When I don't call her back, her message the following week twacks me in the heart.

"We'll air the show on Mother's Day."

"I . . . need time," I say when I call back. "I'll think about it."

My first return to my prison left me with so many treasures, like a vase filled with clear water sweet with a most precious bouquet inside. I needed to absorb my experience, take in its scents, take time to lift each flower, examine it up close and pull its petals apart. I needed time to metabolize what felt like a dream.

"I . . . need time," I say. "I'll think about it."

I need to absorb the potency of my return, integrate what I'd stashed in the recesses of my brain for two decades. I'd rediscovered the beginnings of my life inch by inch and felt the love, the renewed bond to my time with my prison mom, but the sweep of stigma about my prison birthplace felt like prickly terrain to tackle. There's no tour guide to explore and cast off stigma and shame the way the officer had as she escorted me around the prison.

I need time.

I still don't feel whole. A lifetime of "I need to know more" and "I still don't feel quite right." Here it is again. I need more and the only place left to turn—the Feds. I have to go to the source. Nothing stops me when I'm on a mission.

After my visit to Alderson, I petition the Federal Bureau of Prisons in Washington, D.C., for my mom's file. One month after I mail my notarized request, a six-pound package of nine hundred pages from the Department of Justice arrives overnight and reveals that before the bureau removed me from prison, I lived with my birthmother for almost a full year. Her cell was my nursery. Her bed, my crib.

The documents also reveal pieces of the story about my foster care and for the first time, I learn I'm officially adopted around age three or four. My parents had custody of me from the time I was two or three, but the courts didn't legally release me to their custody until Margo signed relinquishment papers. She took a few years to do this, but it's not quite clear how many in the documents.

Some of my toddler time finally falls into place. I can't tell how many foster homes I was placed in, and as an adult, I don't remember any of it.

Next in my files I turn to a page which redefines how I think of my younger self. It's from one foster mother to my prison mom.

Dear Margo,
Madlyn Mary is perky and chatty . . .

I lean back in the chair, shake my head. This two-page letter describes me so far removed from the melancholy, mute little girl my family knew.

My prison files make it clear I was a baby who needed decisions from the beginning but I had fewer problems before my adoption. Prison as my birthplace wasn't the problem. Neither was foster care for me. I guess a girl can only have so many mothers. I must've closed the door with too many. The documents help me understand that my birthmother is a deep memory stitched to my back and I can't outrun her or my infancy in prison, or outrun the traumas of my early years after prison.

I flip through the files and cheer "Right on" for my rebel prison mother when I read about her frequent violations, escapades, and antics.

After all the hurt I've inflicted on others, and now with my personal connection to prison, I feel called to give back, to reach out where I'm comfortable, where I feel at home: women's prisons. Something pulls me to return. This time it's not out of curiosity about my roots. This time it's for the women I know could just as easily have been me sitting in a cell for the rest of my life.

I return to Alderson and address the inmates. I share my story with them and it's a natural fit. Who else can return as an adult and tell a story about her prison birth and beyond? I share what I've learned: how life is less what happens and more about what we do with what happens. It's not a new idea, just one that takes practice to believe and live day by day. I use my life as example of how we're all more than the sum of our parts.

Almost every head in the audience nods, inmates and staff alike. The women smile, assure me, show me I'm doing what I'm meant to do. We're all more than the worst things we've ever done, and we can walk out of our history and begin anew whenever we want. I'm proof of this. I use my story to show the redemption made possible by hope. Hope alone won't solve anything but without hope, nothing's possible.

I take myself into a bigger dream, more prisons in New York, California, Connecticut, both coasts, North and South, meeting women who line up to fill folding metal chairs in prison gyms and we share gratitude and shake hands, hug, and dig deep into our souls. Their gratitude moves me like nothing else I've ever known. Some hug me even with the no-touch prison regulation. My heart fills with what I've been able to give and the abundance they've given me.

I'm comfortable standing in a large audience for one of the first times in my life and find it easier than I thought to share myself. I travel from prison to prison across the country and lead basic writing skills and creativity workshops to inmates, thrilled to witness their hidden talents emerge.

Four months into my prison tours, I receive a parcel from the Federal Bureau of Prisons. I open it and pull out a newspaper. It's one of their internal newsletters and right on the front page, there I am. I stare, horrified. No one had asked my permission. I've become their poster girl for the "bad girl gone good." When I manage to read the article without stuffing it back into the envelope, my emotions calm.

The article unveils my rough beginnings and credits my return to speak and write with female inmates as the first program of its kind in the federal prison system. I clutch the newspaper, semi-proud of my birthplace. I don't think I'll ever boast about it. However, I'm not ashamed about where I was born. It's just a place, a little unique, still just a place.

A place I'm private about. Not secretive, but protective about judgment from others. Debates and dialogue abound with potential for prejudice and heated opinions about prison, inmates, the Appalachia Mountains, the South, Jews, adoption, foster care, race, addiction, all threads in the web of my story, all ripe for passionate opinions and judgment. I do best when I step away from judgment.

Most of all I'm protective of my mother in prison, her addiction, her street life, her crimes and many sentences, and also about the details of our time together. Inmates are a class looked down upon by society, and I hold the highest respect for my mother in prison. She's not here to say, "Tell it, tell it all, baby." For both my mothers, Margo and Mother, this is as much their story as mine.

It's my pocket of truth, one I don't want tainted by pubic opinion or publicized into sensationalism.

Other radio interviews pour in about my prison tours and birthplace, about my birth circumstances, along with inquiries from several literary agents and editors who encourage me to weave my life story into a book. I'm not a tell-all kind of person, and also not interested in putting one more motivational book into the market. I love to read them, I just don't want to write the one I'm asked to write.

I sit for hours with pen in hand but the words do not fly in on wings. Rather, I come up with the one sentence which tipped my world: Secret letter reveals heroin-addicted prison birth.

The rest jumbles in my brain and I have no idea how to untangle it. I withdraw from the agent and editor dialogues and after two years pass, several different film producers hear about the woman born in Alderson when Martha Stewart's sentence there creates a media frenzy.

The last thing I want is any part of it and I retreat even more. I'm not ready to claim my escapades in public, nor the fear, rage, and insecurities which puncutated my life's every moment for most of my days.

On my own, without pressure from strangers to write my story, a light goes off. I'm less and less afraid of the dark corners, less terrified of my own story with its twists and turns. I've grown to understand how secrets don't destroy us, it's the keeping of secrets which can kill us. We think we have secrets, but they have us.

Maybe it's time to share the pieces I want the way I want. I don't get much time to face this new insight, though.

It's a few months on from Mother's first chemo treatment. A month before her eightieth birthday, I visit her and can't shake the heartache. Her strong body has withered into a pile of limbs. I've planned a surprise birthday party and wonder if she'll appreciate it in her condition. Dad assures me she'll be okay.

After a year of chemo, Mother's bedridden and in home hospice care. I continue to fly to Chicago every weekend. I massage her feet, read to her. I hold her little hand, the hand of the woman who's stood by me all these years. I nestle at her side and we nap together. On one visit, I lean over her hospital bed, set up against the wall in my father's study, and brush wisps of her chemo-thinned white hair off her fevered forehead.

"Sorry," I whisper.

She turns. Too much for either of us to name what we're sorry about.

"I love you, Pet."

I swallow. I no longer hate her words of love. I revel in them. We weep together. I cry with guilt over all those years of rejecting her, of injuring her spirit. Her tears, I can only imagine, are also for all of our past losses.

The next day Mother and I discuss my surprising desire for children.

"But I'm single right now." My latest relationship has just ended.

"What if I won't be able to follow my creative passions if I have kids?"

"Women have raised children for centuries," she says, "in all kinds of circumstances and all kinds of relationships, single or not."

She smiles and I hug her. She encourages me to do whatever I want. Kids, career, travel, all together.

I suddenly recognize the truth of my Mother. She's a courageous pioneer. She has been one all along. In my judgment as a child, I believed she and Dad had adopted me to boost their liberal image. I guess it helped me block them out.

Mother, ten years older than my father, adopted me when she was in her forties. More than unusual, she adopted a multiracial girl as though she were oblivious to the rarity of the act.

My parents, already outsiders themselves—Jews in academia—marched around with their little brown-skinned girl, innovators in a segregated 1960s America where black, brown, and white never integrated in public.

I want to be brave for her, give her whatever I can.

"Mother, do you ever wonder about that phone call from the police? Do you . . . want to know about those years I disappeared?"

She smiles.

"Thanks. Not really."

Chapter Eighteen

Lost and Found, Then Lost Again

It's Thanksgiving, and for the first time in many years, eight of us gather at my parents' house at the same time: Mother, Dad, my brother, his wife, their three young children, and me. When Mother, confined to her hospital bed, refuses any food, I try to tempt her with a spoon of whipped cream to her lips. She turns her face. I call the hospice nurse after dinner. She arrives, sees Mother, and calls the family together in the hallway outside her room.

"She's close to death."

For some reason, I glance at the clock: 11:15 p.m., the same time the prison documents record as my time of birth. It's the start of a series of synchronicity, which shows up years after her death.

I stroke Mother's hair with one hand and wrap my other around her bony shoulder. Dad stands opposite me, my brother next to him. When Mother lurches and takes her last breath, I wonder: Did she wait to die until I arrived? I lean down close to her ear. "Thank you, Mother. You'll always be with me." I raise my voice. I want to make sure she has heard me. I need her to know how I value her.

Mother's body lies before me, her life gone. The morgue takes an hour to arrive and I covet the time. I kiss her cool cheeks, then massage her feet. I sit at her side and hold her quiet hands, cry, and stop. Cry and stop. As she's rolled towards the door on a gurney, I feel thankful she and I said everything we needed to say to each other before she passed away.

I shadow the attendants. They load her into a body bag, all the life, all the fight in her gone. My mind taunts me with my fight against her, with all she endured for thirty years. How did she wait for me for so long? How did she stand by me through all I did to her?

I want—need—to give her more and she's gone.

Gone.

Hopelessness tries to drag me down into its hole, but I have to prove to myself and Mother my love for her, my respect. A thirty-year stranger to the temple, back in Minneapolis, I attend the daily mourner's service, and sit Shiva for her. For 365 consecutive sundowns, I recite Kaddish, the Jewish prayer for mourning. I hadn't done any one thing in my life for 365 days. My orthodox uncles who taught me the prayer do it for seven days. But I can't—won't—stop. My adherence shocks everyone, including me.

Grief bites and stings. I need to occupy and distract myself. While I might not have the DNA for impulse control, I discover in those first twelve months without Mother I have an extra gene for quirky off-the-wall creativity. I put my nonlinear bouncy brain to good use and invent things, which take my mind away from constant sadness.

I work nonstop with a fount of ideas. Some tank and I don't care. The challenge and creativity make my heart forget for snippets of seconds who I've lost, all I've lost.

I hardly get time to pay attention to my new life, care for myself, and focus on my work. Signs of my father's Alzheimer's begin to surface.

The day my father finds out he is losing his mind, he can't recall two syllable words on the doctor's orders. Table, Walnut, Diving. He says he sees them swim away, first one, then the other two. Words float from a once measured vocabulary, they swim out of the John Donne and Milton critic. After a lifetime of scrutinizing Paradise Lost, he replies, "Alas, I thought as much," when doctors diagnose dementia. It's his dancing companion, this madness, for ten years.

"Don't much like the idea of an existence without my mind," he tells me on one of our visits to the neruologist.

"Toenails," he adds. "After the mind goes there is not much left but toenails."

Thank God for toenails, I thought. At least there's something left.

The scholar melts into a slow drip through stages of childhood. He reads books with the pages turned upside down. He thumps the wall with the palm of his hand next to the elevator button in the lobby of his assisted living building, his face puzzled why the elevator won't respond to his wall banging.

This part of my story is also the beginning of my life as a mother, a few years before my father dies. Motherhood never seemed possible in my former life. How could I raise children and care for others when I couldn't care or take care of myself? My children are still young as I began to write this, and my belief is their story is for them to tell, which they've confirmed.

Like any parent, I'm protective of their feelings. My world doesn't have to be their world. I'll include them in my public world when the time is right for them.

Pained and fascinated at the same time as I witness the curse of my father's Alzheimer's, I'm shocked his regression parallels the same stages of development as my now seven-year-old daughter.

The disease steals his critical intellectual style but as the intellectual professor fades, Dad softens. We become a little closer before he passes away because I like him better with his tender side, even if it's in dementia.

This part of my story is the beginning of my life as a mother, a few years before my father dies. Motherhood never seemed possible in my former life. How could I raise children and care for others when I couldn't care or take care of myself?

My children are still young as I began to write this, and my belief is their story is for them to tell, which they've confirmed. Like any parent, I'm protective of their feelings.

My world doesn't have to be their world. I'll include them in my public world when the time is right for them.

I'm not prepared for the pressures of parenting. Frustration about something I can't remember erupts one day when I'm alone. I strike the edge of the crib and fracture my right hand. While I never even dream of hitting my girls or anyone else, will I ever stop fighting myself, with the world? I want to be done with this. In a cast for months, I'm back into a counselor's office to get help. Deep rage and fear spin in the air around my head when I least expect it, even though the incidents are years apart. Healing and personal growth are an ongoing venture, never a perfect end in sight.

When my girls go to elementary school, I arrange play dates and sleepovers for them. We pile together and zoom down the slide and then I push them sky high on the rope swing at the park. I sit in parent-teacher conferences and feel clueless.

I've switched from an addict outlaw to a hands-on mom. I monitor Facebook usage and PG movies. I take my daughters to enjoy the Veiled Lady at the Art Institute and hope Mother has come with us. We hold hands and even though I have my two daughters, I long for my mama.

Our family meals are sit-down, all-together affairs, not as formal or long as my childhood dinners, but long enough to sit together and talk. I just grin when other moms at the school ask how I've taught my children such disciplined study habits. I have no idea how, only why: I'm haunted that my kids might run wild like I did.

One afternoon, I pick up my daughters from school.

"We're going to Mexico."

They both jump forward in their seats, eyes aglow.

"When?" they ask.

"Now."

They yelp all the way to the airport and the beam never leaves my face. How life can change. My last visit to Mexico, I had a car full of weed, bags of coke, and a switchblade under the seat. I never thought I'd say it, but now I have something much more precious than drugs in my car.

Chapter Nineteen

On Stage

For the once mute girl who shunned attention, I begin a career as a public speaker. I accept requests to give keynote speeches at conferences for my former enemies, law enforcement and corrections personnel, as well as for professionals in mental health, social work, adoption, foster care, and other social services. The invitations to speak make me reflect and better understand my own journey.

Before I began public speaking, I had not given much thought to how I changed or how much I had changed. I simply progressed through my adult life much like I jumped from a wall as a child or escaped down my tree house or ran from the police—without a plan or foresight. As usual, I followed ideas without any thought to process or consequences.

I only knew that I wanted to change and needed to or I'd die, kill someone, or end up in prison for life. I changed by putting one foot in front of the other and aiming for my target—even when it moved, even when I didn't know the target other than 'anything but here.' It's my "Get me out of here!" instinct, the fight and flight. Now I put it to good use.

Most of all, I present myself as proof that anyone can overcome obstacles. With caution, I tug the crime and drug saga out of my pinhole pocket, along with the family stories. I talk about how I made it out alive, resilient, reinvented. Once again I'm a "poster-girl," but this time I'm an example of what the other side looks like for a child once considered "at-risk and special needs."

Sometimes I share the stage with child psychologists, and from them I learn about early childhood trauma and how it over-stimulates and enlarges the part of the brain—the amygdala—that controls impulses and processes memory of emotions. All my multiple broken attachments and severed bonds as a baby overdeveloped my fight or flight or freeze instinct.

I also learn heroin-exposed infants have hypersensitivity to light, sound, and touch. Researchers debate whether this sensory processing disorder lasts into childhood. I know it lasts into childhood and beyond. It helps explain the occasional pinball of language and sound inside me. At times it's too much for me to drive and talk at the same time, and other times sound and light bounce in a battle for my attention in a group conversation or highly interactive meeting. When it happens, if I can, I excuse myself and struggle to regain focus and balance through breathing techniques.

I focus most on my prison tours and formed a nonprofit organization, the unPrison Project, to embody the work. My work as a speaker is not a verb. It's a social justice and spiritual act. I enter women's prisons to share corners of my soul, to say face to face: I believe in you, your possibility, and the future of your children. Here's what works for me. Let me tell you a story.

More and more after every prison visit, I'm disconnected from everything I know the first days after my return home. A new kind of emotional lockdown. I'll play a little on Facebook, Twitter, and my other social media playgrounds because I can't focus on anything else. My writing, my art, my family and friends—my world— floats far away from me. I struggle to integrate my worlds, my private day-to-day with the intensity of my public life, and most of all, the fierce nature of my prison work. I struggle to find balance, to shift back and forth between my life of writing, family, and friends, and the power and passion I build with women inside prisons.

Therapists estimate that ten percent of a client's "stuff" sticks to the therapist. The stories, the energy, the problems. While I'm not a therapist, I can only imagine what soaks into me with each prison as I leave. Not just the energy from the hundreds and hundreds of inmates, but also the stories of their families and communities, and also from staff and management. Overall, what I've collected from dozens of prisons and thousands of incarcerated women could fill a warehouse, a city, a world of other women's trauma, sorrow, and loss. My work now is to turn into more of a sieve and make sure I renew myself in between each prison tour.

It's a crazy feeling, the tug between these two worlds, so I get grounded in my day-to-day world the best I can before I go out again. Then I download after each prison trip: sleep, read, workout, play with my children, engage with friends and family, also just sit and do nothing.

Sometimes I need weeks to acclimate and shift between my public and private world and sift through what's always traumatic—inside any prison. I do whatever it takes to ground myself as soon as I get out.

Just as it worked when I left my old lifestyle, I use my body to rewire my brain. Yoga, weight lifting, rollerskating, and every way I can think to play helps me shift gears, but half the time I forget I need to do this until I'm in such emotional lockdown and then it strikes me: Do something or else go crazy and explode with the weight of all things. It's not much of a choice and so far, I've chosen to take care of myself rather than explode. It's one of the hardest things to follow, to do the right thing when tugged in a different direction.

Chapter Twenty

Break On Through to the Other Side

Last year, everywhere I turned, up popped my prison mother's name. Martha or her nickname Margo. Day after day she appeared.

Why would she follow me? She's dead now. Why stalk me with her name?

It started in August 2010 right before another trip to my birthplace.

My first encounter with the Marthas started with several Facebook friends with the same name, Margo, Martha, or some derivative. Then one day a census worker calls me to clarify my form, another question about my multiracial category. The census worker's name: Martha.

A few days later I call the phone company with a question. A woman answers. "Hello, my name is Martha. How can I help you?" I almost slam the phone down from the shock of this coincidence, the synchronicity.

When I first wrote about the Martha name synchronicity on my Huffington Post blog, a long-time friend emailed me. "I didn't want to tell you when we first met a decade ago," he said, "but after I read your blog post, I need you to know. You look like my older sister, Martha."

Right about now, I'm in disbelief. "Is this really happening?" I wondered.

The tenth or so Martha, I thought: This is no coincidence!

Once again, she surfaces. A long-time mentor, a dear friend, emails me after she read my Martha blog. "I don't need to tell you my mother's name. Yes. It is."

"That's enough!" Enough of this conspiracy, as if my prison mother stalks me from the beyond.

Could this then serve as a message from her cosmic energy, her way to say: "Notice me. Here I am." The opposite of me, one more introverted and private, I've heard from family members that Margo loved attention.

Maybe sometimes the dead need to be heard.

I've never turned to religion to explain any uncertainties about life, death, and whatever's before and after. My adoptive family is Jewish. I consider myself deeply spiritual in alignment with the energy of our universe.

I'm more inspired to live in the question. I'm drawn to mystery and the unknown, fascinated by all the ways people worship. I've attended everything from services where people speak in tongues to Catholic mass in Latin, from Baptist churches and Jewish temples to parking lot soapbox services. I'm even curious about snake handling as an outcast religious practice.

Nothing in my spiritual exploration explains this chorus of Marthas. In moments of acceptance, I sense a light, an energy cast around me and inside. It's the presence of a wide beam of radiance as if it flows through a tunnel in and out of my core, a direct surge into and from the universe. I know, this is kind of out there, but then so is being born in prison.

My head and heart still spin as I metabolize this mysterious recurrence. Could this fluke of many Marthas not be a coincidence at all? In the spin, I've wondered: Is this my prison mother's way to bless me, bless my journey?

Maybe it's her energy effort, her spiritual way to enter into me. A shared divine breath.

Maybe it's her way to participate in my life. Maybe, despite her transgressions she wanted to give me a new start, to free me from her boxes and labels. Could be this is why she refused to identify the races of my birth father, although it only takes looking at my skin color and ethnic features to know I'm mixed . . . mixed something. She wanted me to be someone who would transcend color, creed, or race. I believe I was her hope for all the disappointment and empty promises she received in her life. I was her future, her hope, her perfection. Just as most parents desire for their children, she wanted a better life for me.

Maybe the Martha occurrences were her way to bless me on my quests as I go home—my birthplace as a passageway now into prison after prison after prison to meet women who share her painful story. A quest I never planned, never imagined.

Could this be Margo's reparation for her part in the wounds of my prison birth, my early heroin exposure, and at the same time for her own healing? I've decided to attempt gratitude, to feel thankful that my prison mother gave me this story and this platform to stand on. I'm now waiting for the gratitude to, "break on through to the other side," as the Doors' song goes.

Even though I expect this synchronistic energy to appear in significant waves throughout my life from now on, I'm still surprised each time. Just the other day, an assistant warden emailed me with a request to speak in her state's prison for women. Yes, her name is Martha. Of course, what other name?

It seems just as Mother walks with me all the time, so does Margo and Martha in this universal quest—the search for home, a place where we are each safe, at home within ourselves. I believe this "Martha walk me home" path confirms for me the concept: we are spiritual beings in a human experience.

I wish I could say I embrace this chorus of Marthas all of the time. I don't. Sometimes I wish she'd send a more fairytale-like missive. Why not set paper lanterns to sail through the skies in my direction, or float lotus blossoms across the seas to reach me? I believe in myths more than I believe in messages from the beyond.

Maybe it's time I change my beliefs.

Chapter Twenty-One

Even Tough Girls Wear Tutus

More than anything, I'm curious. I look for humor and fun in my life as much as I search for purpose and serious meaning.

I get much of this from my parents, especially my mother, the one who adopted me out of foster care, the mother who gave me the encouragement and the courage to live with curiosity. She gave me life in another way, while not by birth, by her gift of curiosity. From her I learned to love whimsy and adventure. I learned about the vitality of joy in the moment.

When I couldn't engage with people in my childhood depression, my mother never gave up. She urged me to notice the world around me, to look for the beauty in everyday life. Together, curiosity and the thrill of adventurous living push me through loss and uncertainty into contentment and joy.

Only recently, years after my mother's death, do I hear her again. "Look around," she'd say on Sunday drives to the Japanese garden in Seattle. She'd call attention to the quiver of the dry grasses in a breeze. She encouraged me to pay attention to details around us on the times she joined excursions with my father to shop at the public market on Seattle's waterfront. "Look at that red on the pomegranate," I remember her saying. Or "Do you like this texture?" and she'd pick up an artichoke.

She'd wrap her arm on my shoulder and lean to watch birds squabble and peck for crumbs at the market entry.

I recall one day when we walked through the homeless park by the market, she pointed out the beauty of lines in an old woman's hands, folded across her lap. At the same time my mother offered some compassion, I learned another lesson from her about inequities in life.

I'd toss a begrudging glance at whatever she suggested, then again hang my head and stare at my feet. I'm surprised I'm not hunched over after all my childhood years of scouring the ground.

Just in recent days I remember her letters during the ten or so years I was estranged from my parents when I moved out at age seventeen. She'd write in her miniscule fountain pen script, "Send me a note, write anything. Tell me what the sky looks like at night or about the fall leaf colors."

I can't pinpoint the exact moment when I started to "look around," but over time, my view of the world changed from that of an angry, fear-filled woman into a woman with insatiable curiosity.

Curiosity replaced my life of drugs, crime, and thrill-seeking. Curiosity gives me the thrill and adventure I need. It's this curiosity about the world and other people, this need to get outside of myself, which saved me. Rather than be apathetic about my surroundings, I focus on the next best step, excited about the unknown even when I'm afraid of it. Whatever it is, I take a step. Doing nothing but glom onto the past saps out more life force than a step, whether it's forward or even a step to the side or backward.

Like no one I've ever met, my mother's curiosity and eagerness to know more, about anything, set the stage for what I teach my children today. Little did my mother know how, once I shed my shell, I'd break out so far.

I thank my mother for this wisdom and freedom, a woman who allowed the tension of opposites to live in me. I thank my prison mom for the spirit of this tug of opposites and how it stirs in me. Each mother, in a different way, taught me to embrace life.

From my prison mother, beyond the addiction I inherited, past the year in prison, I carry a restless, wild fire in my soul, which I'm sure was hers as well. This brought nothing but trouble for years. It's also what drives me to push others and myself with an unquenchable urge to take risks and to break rules or make my own.

Sometimes we need new rules. It's this drive, coupled with an insatiable curiosity, which led me to the world of all things tutu. Some of my tutu mania started with my love of dance and theater, but mostly it's about the tutu as a symbol of freedom and the need to grab life, live it how we want, and when we want, no matter what others think.

I've always adored kooky design and one day I crafted my own tutu to wear over jeans with cowgirl boots. I worked at my desk in my tutu, ate dinner with the family in it, watched the news, and talked on the phone with an editor. All in a tutu.

Then I ventured out into the world: the park, the farmers' market. That's it so far. Why not wear a tutu just for the fun of it? Wear it to pay the electric bill online or when you're on hold for hours at the mercy of the phone company's customer service. With tights, boots, flip-flops, or barefoot; all around the house or out in the yard. Who cares where and how? About anything we wear, any personal truth. Who cares? The tutu is about how to dump our preconceived notions and try on new ones, new ideas.

Yes, even a former tough girl loves a tutu. Fierce and frill all in one. I named it the Tough Girl Tutu. As with my other entrepreneurial ventures, I started to dream and write The Ten Commandments of the Tutu:

1. Let your world stand on four things: Justice, peace, curiosity, and the truth of the tutu.
2. Let it ruffle. Who cares if you're the only one?
3. Honor the spirit of your tutu more than the tutu itself.
4. Tutu does not the woman make, but it does build the power of her dreams.

5. Walk humbly in the grace of your tutu as you would anything else which brings you cause for celebration.
6. Rejoice not in the fall of another's tutu. Instead, offer to pick it up.
7. You shall bear witness to the integrity of the tutu, even if it's not for you.
8. Do not judge another until you have stood in her tutu.
9. If you covet your neighbor's tutu, do it with love and tell her so.
10. Look for the divine sense behind the whimsy of the tutu.

The tutu is my metaphor for the power of paradox, the tension of opposites in this ride of life. The tutu represents what so many of us grapple with: how to turn a rough past into a gentle future. While my prison story is extreme, who doesn't face the tug of conflict and opposition at one time or another?

I've had to wrestle with my prison roots and all that followed my whole life. Wrestle to redefine and re-think my identity.

Don't we all tweak our identity a bit as we go along? A new relationship, marriage, divorce, death, birth, adoption, financial or job change, a move to a new city—every life cycle is also a chance for personal transformation. I learned the hard way as I dismantled myself, brick by brick, until I could look through a new lens, one which took decades to reframe after I'd read the letter and drank the kool-aid of secrecy and shame and committed emotional suicide.

My eleven-year-old daughter finds her own wisdom about the tutu and her mama in one. "It's a little bit out of the ordinary," she said one day when I picked her up after school, the tutu nestled in a pile on the car seat next to her. "I think it means you're spiritually free."

We live with imprisonment of all kinds and life's bumps call for every bit of grit and guts we have. This tulle of rustles and ribbons for me represents a potential for play, freedom, and curiosity, along with grit and courage.

Mothers—we love them, we hate them. No matter what relationship, whether we are a mother or not, no one escapes a mama-connection, even when we try, like I did, and go as far as to plot murder.

Both mothers gone now, sometimes I ache for their presence. Although I'm not sure how either would like my tutu mania. But that's okay because my two young daughters reap the benefits of their mama in a tutu, all part of what I now know makes the bumps in life easier to ride. A combination of play and purpose, creativity, curiosity, honesty, whimsy, and adventure help transform uncertainty into a balance.

I brainstorm, storm my brain, dream it, do whatever it takes to find my way through doubt and uncertainty. I try to dance with the uncertainties in my life instead of attempting the impossible, to stomp it all out. It saved my life, this view of the world through curious eyes. Curiosity and creativity turned deep and unimaginable loss into acceptance, turned sorrow and uncertainty into endurance and productivity.

Like everything else, I discover whatever I need to make life liveable. If not, what I need often finds me. Seems things go like this—what we need, finds us.

Epilogue

What we imagine about an event means as much as what actually happened.

Today I envision my first twelve months in Alderson Prison as a yearlong slumber party. Two hundred incarcerated women, a warden, and me. One long sleepover. My heart sparks when I think of my mom in prison and our bond, even though I have no conscious memory of her. She is in me and our short life together lives deep in my soul.

Sometimes my brain will flash an image of this raw truth, one I still don't believe at times—I was born in prison. How can this be? Panic rises in my gut. I shudder and fight to shake it from my being. But I cope because I've grown, shed the shackles of fear and guilt, secrecy and shame. No longer do I need to destroy myself or blame innocent people and lash out at the world for my losses. Some events scar us but they don't need to define us. Rather than fight my way through life with hate, resentment, and remorse, I've learned to dance with the uncertainties and accept what I can never reconcile.

I now know the truth: I was just in the wrong place at the wrong time.

Or was I? My roots in Alderson tie me to my prison mom. That and probably my high-spirited nature. Or did I get this from Mother with her passionate love of life? Nature and nurture dance in a fierce pas de deux inside me, something between rave and ballet, and sometimes both at once.

I continue to live with uncertainty, still in search of information about my birth father and which boxes to check for race other than Multiracial. I've now discovered through DNA tests I'm part Taiwanese. Add that to Greek and Latina, plus—as my prison documents revealed—a possible "one drop of blood," the archaic law regarding who's considered black. From several reports, when prison authorities requested my prison mom disclose my birth father's identity after speculation he might be biracial, she refused and thus left me with a lifetime of unknowns. I can either battle or embrace this mystery, it depends on how I view it.

Now, rather than an outcast, I'm a perfect palette of paints, part of the new multiracial demographic where one in five Americans will be multiracial by the year 2050.

Danger waits in the shadows for me, though. Not long ago, at the top of a steep hill, I hop on the back of my daughter's kick-scooter and promise her a thrill ride we'll never forget. We're laughing in the wind. I don't think about us not wearing helmets. Worse, we're in t-shirts and shorts. As we careen towards the bottom, the brake doesn't engage and we're in for it if a car enters the intersection. I envelop her body with mine to pitch us off the death trap. My back turns into a skateboard as I protect my girl and we're both scraped and bloody in the emergency room afterward, a road burn all along one side of my body. She's eight at the time, and I'm supposed to know better.

I work hard to catch up emotionally, equally in a struggle to rein in my rebellion when it rises. Sometimes I'm successful, sometimes not. Still an adventure-seeker with a too-high threshold for risk, it's a fight. Every scar leaves scar tissue. When my old brain impulses wiggle inside like a kitty snarled in a blanket, my new lessons push to win the tug of war. It doesn't always prevail. But I'm happy to look at how far I've come instead of the distance ahead.

I keep at it. After all, I've always enjoyed a good challenge. Instead of devoting precious time in a fantasy about what could have been, I focus energy on appreciation for what I have, and look for how I can use my unique gifts, skills, and unusual story to reach out and contribute to a better world, and discover ways to make myself a better person.

The day after Mother's death, I open her cedar trunk and dig through her linens to rescue my toy yarn dog. Packed deeper in the trunk I discover more of Margo's knitted craftwork from her prison workshops—three baby sweaters, one in sunshine yellow with fuzzy pom pom tassles. Reclaimed at last, pieces of our early bond, evidence of her love for me.

I've come to recognize identity as whatever we make for ourselves. Today on top of an ornate scrolled wall sconce in a main hallway in my home, I display the yarn dog next to Mother's Mont Blanc fountain pen, the one she used to write poetry. Symbols of my once fractured self now united side by side. Down the hall from the sconce, I've draped one of my tutus as a wall hanging on a picture hook.

That's me, a tapestry of all, every battle worth the exploration, every bit of confusion worth the contentment and joy I've learned to mine out uncertainty.

To embrace fate, our own nature, is one of life's hardest challenges. But I can't think of anything else we're born to do.

Connect with Deborah

Facebook:
facebook.com/deborah.jiang.stein

Twitter:
@deborahdash

Get Involved

The unPrison Project: Freedom on the Inside
A 501(c)3 nonprofit
theunprisonproject.org

The Facts

The facts are compelling, and they speak for themselves:

- 2.3 million minor children, most under age 10, have a parent in prison. This translates into 3% of all children in the United States.
- Last year, over a quarter million babies were born drug-addicted.
- 50% of heroin babies do not survive birth.
- 75% of women in prisons are mothers. 2/3 have children under age 18.
- 85% of incarcerated women are in drug and alcohol abuse programs.
- Over 1 million women are imprisoned, about 1% of the U.S. female population.
- Women are the fastest growing prison population. The number of women in prison in the United States increased by 832% over a 10 year period (between 1977 and 2007.)
- 4-7% of women entering prison are pregnant.
- The majority of women are sentenced for nonviolent drug related crimes.

- Nearly all women in prisons have experienced abuse of one kind or another: sexual, psychological, or emotional
- The United States has the largest prison population in the world. With 5% of the world's population, the U.S. houses nearly 25% of the world's reported prisoners.

Facts gathered from Department of Justice and Bureau of Justice statistics.

Discussion Guide

Even Tough Girls Wear Tutus is a story about the rise of hope and possibility in the face of adversity and battling personal demons. This story raises the questions: Is there any such thing as a bad life story, or just a bad way to view it and tell it?

This is the tale of how one woman, born in prison, prevails after more than a twenty-year fight against the world in her struggle to accept her roots, herself, and her family. Her ability to rebound is an affirmation of the capacity for everyone to reframe her story, transform, and not only overcome adversity but also find joy and contentment while still living with irreconcilable fragments.

The following themes weave throughout *Even Tough Girls Wear Tutus*:

- Secrecy and shame in everyday lives.
- How to find the courage to face obstacles and live a life with purpose.
- Imprisonments outside of jails and prisons: uncertainty, fear, loss, doubt.
- We don't always end up where we thought we were headed. Everyone has permission to fail, take risks, and open up to positive change.

- Personal transformation and resilience.
- Influences of nature and nurture.

Discussion Questions

1. The author writes about when she learned of her birth in prison and struggles to grasp the severity of her beginnings. Do you remember a time in your life when you were surprised to find out something about yourself others already knew?

2. Discuss if some secrets are best kept a secret, or if it is always better to bring them out in the open.

3. The tug of multiple identities is one theme in this book. Where has this shown up in your life?

4. Adoption is a popular topic in the news and also a current celebrity trend. What are your thoughts on celebrity trans-racial adoptions and trans-racial adoption in general?

5. Throughout this memoir, the author struggles with her issues of nature and nurture. Discuss if one dominates the other, and if a person can suppress one and cultivate the other.

6. The incarceration rate for women has risen 800 percent in the last ten years, making women the fastest growing prison population. Most women, like the author's birthmother, are imprisoned for non-violent crimes. What alternatives would you propose besides incarceration?

7. At the time of this publication, eleven prisons house nurseries for newborns to women in prisons.

Discuss whether a child who stays with her mother in prison is being unfairly punished and sentenced herself, given the restrictions and deprivations of prison environments. Should these children be allowed to bond with the mother or be removed as soon as practical and placed in adoption, foster care, or with the mother's extended family?

8. Despite everything, the author eventually reconciled with her parents, accepted her prison roots, and found peace within her. In this book, what was the turning point or points? Who helped her along the way? Talk about the steps taken toward reconciliation and redemption.

9. Some people, when faced with obstacles or adversities, give up while others fight. Throughout the book, the author wrestles her way through one challenge after another. What qualities do you think enable a person to overcome obstacles?

10. The author's strength of curiosity and perseverance carry her through life's challenges. What's your inner strength?

11. The author reveals a series of several "second chances" she's encountered. What's been your second chance?

12. In this story, the tutu symbolizes an opportunity for the author to explore what restrains her, and where and how she finds the courage to discover a feeling of liberty. Discuss one thing you've always wanted to do but haven't yet done. What holds you back, and why don't you do it? What will it take for you to do it?